NATURE, WILDLIFE AND HUMAN RACE

Dr. S.K. Singh
Professor & Head
Department of Wildlife Management
Faculty of Forestry
Birsa Agricultural University
Kanke, Ranchi - 834 006 (Jharkhand), India

Published by

Khushnuma Complex Basement
7, Meerabai Marg (Behind Jawahar Bhawan)
Lucknow 226 001 U.P. (INDIA)
Tel. : 91-522-2209542, 2209543, 2209544, 2209545
Fax : 0522-4045308
E-Mail : ibdco@airtelmail.in

First Edition 2010

Price: Rs. 110/-

ISBN 978-81-8189-473-1

Composed & Designed at :
Panacea Computers
3rd Floor, Agrawal Sabha Bhawan
Subhash Mohal, Sadar Cantt. Lucknow-226 002
Phone : 0522-2483312, 9335927082
E-mail : prasgupt@rediffmail.com

Printed at:
Salasar Imaging Systems
C-7/5, Lawrence Road Industrial Area
Delhi - 110 035
Tel. : 011-27185653, 9810064311

Dedicated
to
Almighty

- Author

PREFACE

Nature is full of miracles and it balances all its creatures in very wisely, nicely and scientifically manner. Its way of management and conservation is in such a way that eco-balance is maintained automatically so that its each and every creature may live and breathe in healthy and hygienic conditions. But the modern man, the supreme intelligent ruler of this earth planet, himself is a great manipulator of the system for his convenience and comfort due to short sightedness without realizing the consequences in the long run. From the very beginning of our culture and civilization, human race was living together very hormonally with all the other creatures, particularly with the wildlife, of the nature by showing ethnic approach. But in course of time; as our modernization started growing and growing, greedy and short-sighted persons began to exploint the natural resources like forests and wildlife. Since wildlife is one of renewable natural resources, it must be used judiciously in scientific manner otherwise it would lead to disastrous condition giving rise to ecological imbalances because it plays an important role in eco-balance through food-chain and food-web to which human race is also a part.

Today, we are passing through 21st century and claim for very high development in the ladder of civilization; it is unfortunate that the general human mass is not conscious and aware about the role played by the wildlife. That's why, wild animals are facing illegal hunting, killing, poaching, smuggling and habitat destruction by greedy and unawared people and have been brought to face the alarming stage of extinction. We are losing their number and existence day by day. There are so many reasons behind it; illiteracy, lack of awareness, poverty, over-population and unemployment being the major ones. We cannot imagine progress in conservation measures and practical applications of strictness of law until these problems are solved at mass scale. And the day is not far, if the situation goes like this unchecked, when we will have nothing in our hands facing the stage of the annihilation. Though, legally there is a ban on hunting of wild animals in our country; but practically the situation is different and therefore, intellectuals as well as government are compelled to think over methodologies to overcome such problem in better a way so that conservation and protection of wildlife could be ensured. This can be done by enhancing their population by applying wildlife management techniques in a scientific way, not only upto carrying-capacity but also beyond it to obtain revenue from them.

Keeping these views in mind, I have been inspired to write the present book mentioning and coating relationships of human race with the wildlife/wild animals. If it creates awareness and consciousness among general mass towards conservation and protection of the wild animals, I will feel myself grateful not only to the society but also to the wild animals who are mute, innocent and helpless. They sometimes become violent because when anybody destroys one's house, it is obvious to resist the move.

I would like to express my thanks to my family members who always encouraged and cooperated in bringing this holy and noble work to fruition.

Lastly, although every attempt has been made to do away with the anomalies in the book, suggestions about the book itself and the mistakes that may have crept in its writing or printing will be highly appreciated.

- Author

सर्वेषामेव दानानामिदमेवैकमुत्तमम् ।
अभयं सर्वभूतानां नास्ति दानमतः परम् ।।

पद्म पुराण

"Of all the gifts only one is supreme.
It is the freedom from fear.
For all the creatures of this universe.
There is no other gift greater than this."

CONTENTS

Chapter 1

Wildlife As A Renewable Natural Resource

The Nature is full of miracles. It maintains its system (ecosystem/eco-balance) very nicely, wisely and judiciously in a well-planned manner. If not disturbed, it provides its natural resources to each and every creature including man in perpetuity to lead sustained and smooth life on this planet maintaining harmony and natural-balance. As we know, sun is the main source of energy for this planet. The green plants use this energy to prepare food for all other organisms on this earth by the process of photosynthesis. Thus, green plants convert solar energy into chemical energy which is stored in plants. Animals also get their energy from plants. Therefore, all living organisms directly or indirectly depend on the sun as the source of energy. The Nature has gifted us varied and marvellous forms of wildlife in the form of renewable natural resources as heritage. It is our duty to conserve and manage it in such a way that we can get sustained yield in perpetuity from it to lead our life in a smooth way in healthy atmosphere from generation to generation. We, the men, are the main agent to disturb or manipulate the nature (natural habitats) disturbing eco-balance and ultimately ourselves, as we are part of the system.

India is very rich in biodiversity including wildlife. It has a variety of wild animals that automatically draw the man's attention giving a pleasant feeling. As far as resources are concerned, all the substances used by man for sustenance and welfare are called resources. Man is dependent on plants and animals. The plants and animals, in turn, are dependent on natural substances like air, water, soil, minerals etc. All such resources existing in nature are called as natural resources. Natural resources are of two types :-

Renewable Natural Resources: The resources which are generated through natural cycles such as forests, plants, animals, soil, water, sunlight, wind, air etc. These resources are generated in nature but among them some are exhaustible like soil, groundwater, forests, plants and animals whereas some are inexhaustible like sunlight, wind and water. In this context, we are concerned with wildlife which stands under the category of exhaustible resources. If its management, conservation and uses are not proper and judicious; it may exhaust after some time. Wildlife is renewable only if indiscriminate hunting and unscientific exploitation is prevented.

Non-renewable Natural Resources : Those which are not replaced in the environment after their utilization such as metals, coal, natural gas, minerals etc.

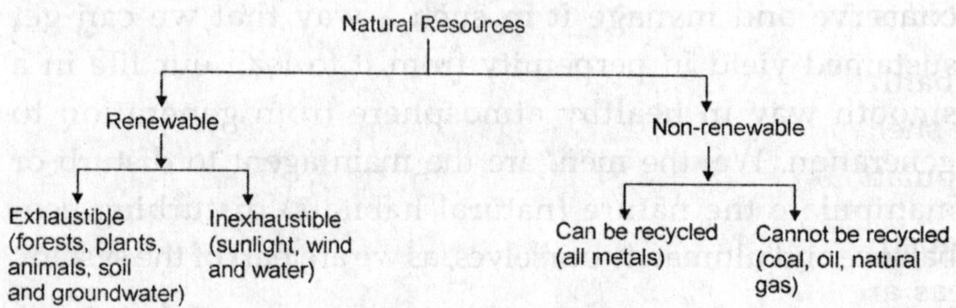

Hence, man has to be very careful and cautious in using these natural resources both renewable and non-renewable to get maximum benefit in perpetuity from them. Killing of one species may cause considerable disturbance in the food-chain and food-web and thus may upset other species. In the long term, these changes may also affect man.

Wildlife includes all plants and animals that are not domesticated but in strict sense, they are the undomesticated animals specially mammals, birds, reptiles and fishes which are generally hunted. Due to over-exploitation and encroachment of forests and habitats of wildlife, many plants and animals have become extinct and many are on the verge of extinction.

Causes of depletion of resources :

The major causes of depletion of resources are as mentioned below :

Over population - Due to tremendous growth in human population, the demand of natural resources is increasing at an enormous rate. Simultaneously, poverty and unemployment help enhance of encroachment of wildlife habitats, deforestation, illegal hunting and so on. Alternative solid engagement to the people specially living around such habitats must be provided to check and control such activities.

Urbanization - Coming up more and more towns and cities for shelter and other basic needs for ever increasing human population is resulting in depletion of some resources.

Industrialization - New industries in rural as well as urban areas are being established day by day resulting in over-exploitation of natural resources.

Deforestation - Deforestation and encroachment of forests are continuously depleting renewable natural resources like soil, water, wildlife etc.

Mining and Quarrying - Unscientific mining and quarrying for the extraction of minerals and ores are also depleting the resources.

Over-grazing - Over-grazing by cattle, sheep, goat etc. increase soil erosion, decrease vegetational growth and so on.

Use of Pesticides - Pesticides, insecticides, waste products of industries, sewage and town refuse pollute the environment as well as reach the rivers, ponds, dams and ultimately mix up the ocean water. This invariably affect the wild animals as well as human being and also disturbs ecological-balance in nature.

Hunting - Indiscriminate hunting of wild animals is resulting extinction of many species. Wild animals are killed or trapped for their hides and skin, fur, meat, pharmaceuticals, perfumes, cosmetics and decoration purposes.

Though, man's progress in present days is the world is directly dependent on renewable natural resources, we should conserve these resources to make them long lasting for human welfare if we want to make steady and perpetual progress. These resources should be utilized judiciously, wisely and scientifically replacing them whenever necessary without destroying them. Their use should be without causing any ecological imbalance. In this way, the scientific management of wildlife is to maintain it at its optimum level and derive sustainable benefit from the present as well as future generations. Wildlife conservation includes protection, preservation and perpetuation of rare and endangered species of plants and animals in their natural habitats. Thus, conservation of living resources has mainly three objectives, viz, -

- to maintain essential ecological processes and life-support systems.
- to preserve the diversity of species or the range of genetic material found in the world's organisms.
- to ensure sustainable utilization of species and ecosystems which support general mass and industries.

Thus, conservation of living resources is concerned with plants, animals and micro-organisms with non-living elements of the environment on which they depend. For the purposes, scientists of the world have evolved "World Conservation Strategies" for the judicious use of resources. The national protection programmes have to be coordinated tightly with the international programmes like MAB, IUCN, IBWL, CITES, WWF etc. related to Protected Areas such as national parks, sanctuaries, biosphere reserves etc. Various wildlife organizations (GOs & NGOs) are playing their role in this regard.

After studying the impact of human-interference causing changes in the environment/ ecosystem, it is the duty of every citizen to conserve the natural resources and natural environment to lead a healthier life in future.

preservation and perpetuation of rare and endangered species of plants and animals in their natural habitats. Thus, conservation of living resources has mainly three objectives, viz.

- to maintain essential ecological processes and life-support systems
- to preserve the diversity of species or the range of genetic material found in the world's organisms
- to ensure sustainable utilization of species and ecosystems which support general masses and industries

Thus, conservation of living resources is concerned with plants, animals and micro-organisms with non-living elements of the environment on which they depend. For the purposes, scientists of the world have evolved 'World Conservation Strategies' for the judicious use of resources. The national protection programmes have to be coordinated rightly with the international programmes like MAB, IUCN, IBWL, CITES, WWF etc. related to Protected Areas such as national parks, sanctuaries, biosphere reserves etc. Various wildlife organizations (GOs & NGOs) are playing their role in this regard.

After studying the impact of human-interference causing changes in the environment/ecosystem, it is the duty of every citizen to conserve the natural resources and natural environment to lead a healthier life in future.

Chapter **2**

Importance and Values of Wildlife for Human Beings

As discussed in the previous chapter, we may just believe and understand, how important and valued for human beings wildlife is. It may be described by the following points :-

1. **Ecological importance -** Wildlife maintains nonetheless balance of nature through -

- regulation of population of different species by the self-regulation and feedback mechanism.
- regulation of food-chains or passage of food and energy through series of populations comprising producers, consumers and micro-organisms (decomposers).
- regulation of natural cycles or circulation of inorganic nutrients between biotic and abiotic environments as well as prevention of leaching and run off.
- preserving the environment as a self-sustaining system, balancing population and maintaining food-chain/food-web and natural cycles.

The most fundamental reason to conserve wildlife is its ecological significance. All animals, both terrestrial and aquatic, play their important role in the maintenance of balance of nature as an intangible value. Since ecology is the relationship between the living things with their environment and wild animals are the part of the nature, they form a complex relationship with it through the dynamic ecosystem and life-support system. As we know, an ecosystem comprises two components such as biotic (all minerals, gases, water etc.) and biotic (plants as well as animals). Green plants are called as autotrops or producers because they manufacture their own food releasing oxygen by the process of photosynthesis. On the contrary, the animals have no such arrangement and thus depend upon the plants directly or indirectly for energy uptaking as food and hence, called as consumers or heterotrophies passing from primary consumers (herbivores) to the carnivores as secondary, tertiary consumers and so on. Lastly, decomposers including bacteria and micro-organisms consume dead and rotten flora and fauna. In this way, there is direct interrelationship between autotrophs and heterotrophs. Abiotic and biotic components of the ecosystem are closely interlinked with each other, and there is continuous flow of energy through the different trophic levels. Therefore, disturbance in any component of the ecosystem, deliberately or not, results in imbalance leading to disastrous condition for nature and ultimately to man himslef because he is also a part of the overall ecosystem. It is clear that wild animals occupy the position of consumer in the cycle of ecosystem. As stated above, herbivorous wild animals feed upon the plants which produce food in nature from sunlight and carbon dioxide in presence of chlorophyll through the process of photosynthesis releasing oxygen. Such plants are known as producers of the ecosystem. The animals which feed directly upon the plants are herbivores and called as primary consumers such as deer, elephant, rabbit etc. The second category of wild animals are carnivores which prey upon these primary

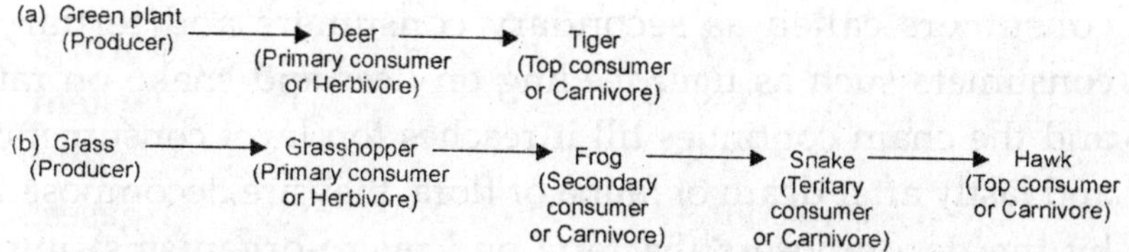

Fig. Showing food-chains (a) Forest ecosystem (b) Grassland ecosystem.

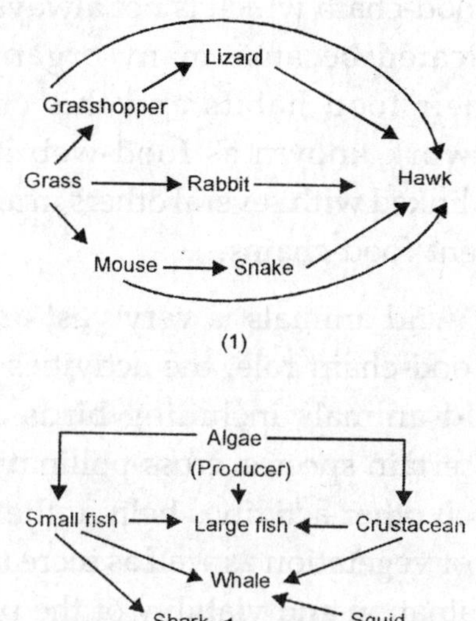

Fig. Showing Food-webs (1) Grassland ecosystem (2) Marine ecosystem.

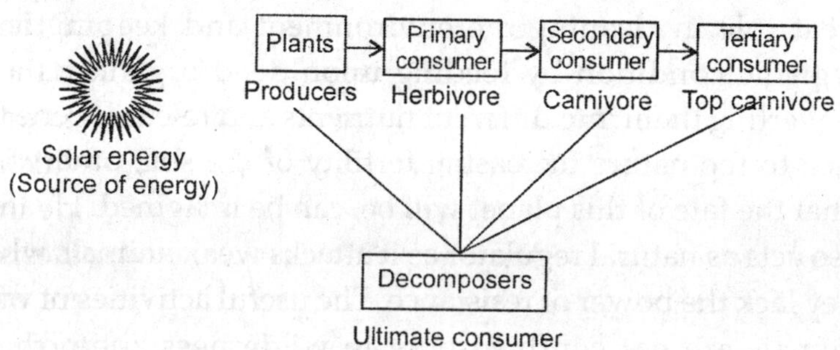

Fig. Showing Trophics of an ecosystem.

consumers called as secondary consumers and tertiary consumers such as tiger feeding on deer and snake on rat and the chain continues till it reaches top level consumers; and lastly after death of fauna or flora, they are decomposed by the decomposers (bacteria and micro-organisms) into abiotic components and thus cycle is repeated continuously. This is called as food-chain which is not always so simple. It is rather complicated because many organisms behave differently in their food habits and this chain forms a complicated network known as food-web in which one organism may be linked with several others in an interlocking manner of different food-chains.

Thus, the role of wild animals is very vast and important. Apart from the food-chain role, the activities like seasonal migration of wild animals including birds and selective feeding habit of certain species, cross-pollination by insects and birds and such other activities help in the development and propagation of vegetation as well as increasing diversity of genetic recombination and viability of the plants. Besides these, some wild animals are natural scavengers such as vulture, eagle, kite, crow, hyaena, jackal, wolf etc. playing great role in cleaning the environment and keeping it in hygienic condition by feeding upon dead organisms and converting them into different nutrients and releasing energy back to the nature increasing fertility of the soil, otherwise, what the fate of this planet will be, can be imagined. Hyaena also acts as natural regulator as it attacks weak animals when they lack the power of resistance. The useful activities of wild animals are not confined only in wilderness zone but in captivity their role is also important as people's entertainment and stimulating interest of love and preservation towards wildlife.

Hence, for keeping the earth planet as a viable platform for healthy life and alive natural activities, it is essential to recognize and apprehend the importance of wildlife. It should be conserved and propagated more judiciously and scientifically than before for rectifying and rehabilitating the eco-balance to save from devastation in it because already destruction of wildlife habitat by reckless tree cutting and ruthless killing of wild animals has threatened ecological-balance changing the environment such as degradation of land, soil erosion, reduction in water level, floods, extinction of so many species and other various climatic anomalies putting question mark on the survival of human race as man himself cannot survive against the law of nature being part and parcel of the ecosystem.

2. **Gene Bank Importance** - For human progress, preservation of wildlife has great significance as gene banks for breeding programmes in animal husbandry, agriculture and fishery. Wildlife serves as a gene bank for breeding improved varieties which comes from the wild relatives. We cannot predict which species become useful to us in future. For example, if penicillium had been eliminated from the earth before man could discover its antibiotic properties or cinchona had become extinct from Peru before quinine was discovered, some of the severest infectious diseases would have continued to savage the world. With increasing knowledge and skills, man is busy finding new uses from traditional species. A species once lost cannot be retrieved. Therefore, it would be unethical to be responsible for the destruction of a species. We have an evolutionary responsibility to conserve biological diversity for our descendants.
3. **Scientific importance** - As we know, wild animals are

used for research purposes and for studies of anatomy, physiology, evolutionary aspect, ecology etc. which help in saving human life. The role of wildlife in the advancement of fundamental sciences and medical sciences is very much important. All over the world, a number of scientists are achieving their scientific goals by studying on wild animals. The invented drug is used and tried first on wild animals to find out its side effects before applying on the human body. We are always learning structures and functions of different animals and their evolutionary trend and realtionship with the nature. Had rhesus monkey not been in natural heritage, we would have not known about R^h factor in human blood, likewise chimpanzee had helped us in conducting sereological protein test and so on. Bat might had been instrumental in discovery of radar and ultrasonic scientific discovery for the modern man. Some of the wild flora and fauna are also of medicinal value benefiting us directly or indirectly, for example, musk pod and musk deer and rhinoceros horn are of great medicinal value, fat of tiger and hornbill is used in rheumatism, snake venom is used for preparing antivenom against snake bite. Thus, it is clear that preservation and propagation of wild animals is very helpful in human welfare. The killing of certain species for scientific purposes must be compensated by propagating and managing them applying scientific technologies.

4. **Cleaning of environment** - As discussed earlier, scavengers and decomposers including micro-organisms feed upon dead animals converting them into nutrients and releasing energy back to the nature to make available to the plants specially autotrophs/producers increasing

fertility of the soil in the ecosystem. In this way, the cycle is going on repeatedly and they are doing very important work in the cleaning of the environment providing us calm and healthy atmosphere to live in, otherwise, fate of this earth planet may just be imagined.

5. **Economic/Commercial importance** - Many products of commercial value are obtained from wildlife such as timber, firewood, paper pulp, gum, resins, tannins, drugs, oils, spices, lac, silk, honey, feather, guano (drug of sea fishes used as manure), leather, musk, ivory, hide etc. In this respect, tiger may be taken as an example providing us different parts of very high value in national and international market (which is totally illegal, and illegal killing of the tiger is going on for such purposes) whose values may be realized in following way -

   Skin - to treat mental illness and as ornamental article.

   Fat - for vomiting, dog bites, bleeding haemorrhoids, scalp ailments in children

   Flesh - for nausea and malaria to improve vitality and tonitying the stomach and spleen and to gain energy.

   Hair - to drive away centipedes when burnt.

   Brain - to cure laziness and pimples.

   Eyeballs - for epilepsy, malaria, nervousness of fevers in children, convulsions and cataracts.

   Nose - for epilepsy and children's convulsions.

   Teeth - for rabies, asthma and sores on the penis.

   Whiskers - for toothache.

   Tail - for various skin diseases.

   Testes - for tuberculosis of the lymph nodes.

Blood - for strengthening the constitution and willpower.

Gallstones - for weak or watering eyes and abscesses of the hand.

Stomach - for controlling upset stomach and convulsions in children.

Benefits are also obtained from tourists, exports and hunting of surplus stock of wild animals. However, killing or taking any type of economic benefit from wild animals or its products is legally banned now a days in our country due to their alarming condition, though in many countries people are earning through trade in this field. Moreover, fishes are a big industry in respect of income and employment. Countries like Africa have shown that in marginal land wild animals are found to be more productive and profitable than the domesticated animals. Hence, our policy should be in the direction of exploiting commercial value from wild animals beyound its optimum density without interfering natural balance under the aims and objectives of wildlife management.

6. **Recreational importance -** Wildlife is of great value in terms of providing recreation to the masses. In developed countries, it is a source of tremendous economical gain linking it with the tourism industry. While we are passing through the age of polluted life curtailing the availability of free air, wildlife inhabiting in nature, national parks, sanctuaries, biological parks, zoos etc. provide us refresh air and relaxation in tension. Recreational Forestry is becoming fast popular day by day in most of the countries of the world. People try to find time from the busy routine of modern life to get some moments of pleasure and mental peace with

wildlife. India has great potential and opportunity of such value of its wildlife keeping varied beautiful, magnificent and majestic wild animals as heritage and requires only efforts and interests in this direction. In U.S.A. and other developed countries, many people spend huge money in hunting and fishing getting revenue from it as well as by selling arms and appliances connected with these 'game work'. Fishing is encouraged in our country also as a sport as well as industry as it has wide scope. Some of the wild animal species like elephant, bear, monkey, mongoose etc. are tamed and used for various purposes. Before advancement of modern transportation methods, the elephants were the main source of carriage and status symbol including battle field.

Apart from the above positive values and importance of wildlife, certain negative values such as destructionof properties, killing of man and cattle, carriers of various diseases etc. are connected with the wild animals. Off and on, there is man-animal conflict (now-a-days in our country, man-elephant conflict is more prominent) for such major mishappenings. Herbivorous animals like deer, elephant, wild ass etc. destroy the agricultural crops and carnivores like tiger, panther, lion etc. sometimes become cattle-lifters causing hardship for the villagers. Sometimes, they become man-eaters also and the elephant being herbivorous in nature also takes human lives by killing. However, the positive values of wildlife is always outweighed than the negative values and the necessity is only to manage their habitats as per their carrying-capacity so that they may remain inside their own habitats happily and peacefully, without harming human beings and their property because such mischievous activities are occurring mainly due to their habitat destruction and shrinkage.

Chapter **3**

Necessity of Wildlife for Human Existence

The life on this planet earth is not simple but in the form of a delicate system of balance of nature. Plants convert carbon dioxide and water into organic matter as food with the help of chloroplasts in the presence of sunlight liberating oxygen also which is necessary for any living organism utilizing in respiratory process. Herbivorous animals derive their energy from the plants and the carnivores in their turn from the herbivores. There are also organisms called decomposers which release energy back to the nature, thus completing the cycle. We, thus, see that producers, consumers and decomposers form food-chains and thus maintain natural-balance. The various food-chains and cycles constitute life-support systems essential for the survival of the living world. Any major alteration in any one of these, results in serious disturbance in the balance of nature leading to annihilation and may threaten the very existence of man himself on this planet. Therefore, to sustain life, renewability of the resources and life-support systems must be maintained for endless duration, which in turn, demands an understanding of the ability of the species to adopt themselves to the changing environment and to integrate these considerations in the development of any planning process. Hence, it is clear that how much important and essential wildlife is, which is renewable part of this life-support system, for human existence and his survival.

The exploitation of the forest as well as wild animals can be said as the main reason of all sorts of problems created by human-interference. Selfish and greedy persons are always busy in taking illegal benefits from the forests and habitats of wild animals causing damage. Some people inhabiting forest areas also indulge in such illegal activities. As a result, both forest as well as wildlife crops are at alarming stage and we are passing through the age of danger. Man is doing illegal hunting of wild animals which is always unscientific. Usually such hunting is by smugglers, local people living inside/neighbourhood of the forest and other greedy persons to make quick money causing heavy loss in wildlife populations. Unless and until such activities are stopped, we neither do proper wildlife management nor achieve our goal. The main reason of extinction and alarming condition (endangered/threatened/rare/on the verge of extinction etc.) of wild animals is illegal /unscientific hunting and destruction/disturbance/shrinkage of habitats. Now about 250 species of wild animals in India are considered as extinct prone species. Assessment of the conservation programmes and policies formulated and implemented over the past 30 years showed that good intentions always yielded the desired results and there have been crisis and disasters of all sorts from all the corners. Now, there is an urgent need to adopt a united and integrated approach to achieve fruitful results. Presently, the major challenges are unprecedented poaching and hunting, illegal trade of animal parts, continuous loss of habitat and forest covers, increasing tourists and traffic inside core wildnerness zones, lack of interstate co-operation, lack of man power and infrastrutural facilities and so on. Another reason of failure of the conservation mission is that there has not seen a co-ordinated attempt of species evaluation to know the status of the species concerned as well as no systematic programme to rehabilitate the major endangered species has been adopted. Even after three decades of conservation march, we are not able to restore the constantly shrinking habitats of the most endangered species and no meaningful conservation programmes have been adopted. It is, therefore, demand of the time that a more cohesive, meaningful and fruitful approach to propagate wildlife conservation is required. There is an immediate necessity to update the knowledge of present status of endangered species alongwith species-specific conservation projects. Though, India has perhaps widest heterogeneity in the world but only 3-4 per cent of forest cover is under Protected Areas as national parks and sanctuaries and fauna are restricted under such small pockets. Hence, to save the endangered species, it is essential to protect and manage their habitats properly understanding their roles in the ecosystem. Therefore, proper hard rule being practically fit and its unbiased implementation is required to control such unlawful activities, but at the same time alternative engagement should also be provided to the local people residing in and around the forest to remove poverty and unemployment and ultimately pressure on the forest and wild animals.

Tremendous growth in human population followed by habitat destruction raises question on advancing technologies and development resulting in "environmental hazard" and putting doubtful existence/future of man. Knowledge of relationship of man/organism with the ecosystem/environment is must for conservation of both human race and natural resources. The man-food relationship is a basic one in studies of human-beings, and so, study and knowledge of interaction of man and biosphere are relevant and necessary. Development of advanced techniques, industries and socio-economic changes on large scale all over the world cause rapid environmental/habitat changes causing pollution and environmental hazard. It is the demand of time giving priority to protect human existence rather engineering and industrial advancement. It is necessary to plan eco-friendly enterprises on natural environment of mankind to cope with ecological relationships, otherwise we will face global danger because pollution does not respect boundaries. We are duty bound to manage our planet very wisely and judiciously for present and future generations to avoid annihilation. Utilization of natural resources for human needs and maintenance of harmony with nature are our great task of studies and understanding. For the purpose, we have to know the place of man in ecosystem and role of forests and wild animals including other natural resources and their interactions aiming linkages with the human existence and maintaining equilibrium (homeostatis of ecosystem); because the environment comprises the overall surroundings consisting of all factors which affect the survival and reproduction of living organisms and elements of environment are building and energy-supplying components and regulatory also, whose presence is essential for the existence of living organisms and the factors regulating those living processes for life-support systems. Protection of the environment is equally important for the development by industry, agriculture, breeding production and so on.

In developing countries like India, the population explosion with poverty and unemployment need much attention and strategies/planning to save and protect habitats in proper way. The main causes of environmental hazards are enormous growth in human population, industrialization, motorization, poverty, unemployment and ultimately habitat destruction (forests etc.) resulting in depletion and alarming condition of wildlife following ecological imbalance.

Since human-ecology is an interdisciplinary branch of science dealing interrelations between man and his environment, it is necessary to determine all over the world the propertis of the environment/ecosystem and the nature as well as the rate of their changes to intensify and justify human, animal and other natural resources. It is necessary to study the direction of changes in organisms of biogeographic conditions of an area or habitat. Overall activities should be with the aim to protect the environment so that we can get food, water and air in perpetuity because there is large gap in our knowledge of the relationships between the environment and man as well as man and wildlife. In this context, strict legislative measures must be followed specially in the field of changes to be brought about in the environment by man which must be acceptable rather drastic and dangerous.

From community point of view, an animal has to protect itself not only against adverse climate but also against its enemies and parasites. It has to compete for its food with fellows of its own as well as other species. Hence, there is an interdependence and interrelationship among animals living together in a particular area calling as animal-association. They are bound together by common interests and living together in particular habitat which is best suited to their needs. They influence each other's lives and by their separate activities contribute in maintaining the community as a whole. For the purpose, there is organization in the community and the relationship among its members. Plants (autotrophs) form the basic food of animals (heterotrophs) in trophic levels of the ecosystems. Hence, in any animal community, plant-eaters form the basic and most numerous class. They are the foundation upon which the communal organization is built up. These plant-eaters (primary consumers) provide food for carnivores (secondary consumers) and make possible existence for them. In this way, a tiger's upkeep is dependent upon the existence of plants, because without plants there would be no deer and other herbivores, and without these plant-eating animals to prey upon, there could be no tigers. Likewise, omnivorous animals (eating both flesh and plant/vegetable food) are also dependent. Apart from these; there are animals that earn their livelihood as scavengers (feeding on the remains of other animals) acting as natural-cleaners keeping the environment in hygienic condition, and some animals like hyaena etc. are acting as natural-regulators feeding weak and unabled animals lacking power of resistance. Finally, there are decomosers (leading life on dead and dying organisms) converting the dead and dying organisms into minerals, gases etc. releasing in the environment to make available to the living organisms, particularly plants, to be recycled and run the system smoothly. In this way; within the community, each animal occupies a particular niche and plays a particular role in the system (ecosystem). The plant-eaters act as a check on the enormous growth of plants and flesh-eaters control the over-increase of the herbivorous species. This results in control of numbers and makes even-distribution of the food-supply, which might be otherwise threatened by the superabundant increase of any one species. For example, the rate of increase is highest among the smaller herbivores, the rodents, for instance, and to counteract this increase in rodents are preyed upon by small carnivores, which themselves have a high rate of productivity. With an increase in the size of the animal, there is a corresponding decrease in the number of young produced, and predators and prey diminish in numbers. Thus, a certain balance of life is maintained within the community as eco-balance. Though; there is fluctuation in increase and decrease in numbers of the animal species with time and season, the margin of increase and decrease is kept within a narrow limits by the law of eating and being eaten and by other checks, unless disturbed or manipulated by decimating factors like flood, drought, epidemics, human-interference etc.

From composition and geographical distribution point of view of the animals in the world, Zoogeographical Distribution gives knowledge of animal life of ancient geography as well as also indicates changes which have taken place in the distribution of land and water, and how the present distribution of land animals has been brought about. As far as distribution of animals is concerned, the most prevalent is its zoo-geographical distribution, however, in addition, they may also be viewed as per the Biomes/Forest Types Distribution for much more understanding and apprehension. Distribution of wild animals in different types of climatic conditions are different as per adaptation acquired by the animals in regard with morphological and anatomical features. This is the reason, some animals are arboreal, some are terrestrial, some are aquatic (fresh water/marine), some have capacity of jumping and running, while some are cursorial, some are diurnal and some nocturnal, some have defensive organs like tentacles, quills, tusks etc., some have water-conserving devices in desert and dry conditions and so on. In this way, the animals have various types of adaptations to suit in the respective environment as per the demand of the climatic condition. The adaptations may be structural, functional, behavioural or a combination of these. As such, animals are full of miracles in varied forms. As stated earlier; in an ecosystem, the physical or nonliving component of the environment (sunlight, air, water and minerals), interacts with the living component of the environment (plants and animals). It is self-contained and self-perpetuating natural system as well as life-support system working as producers, consumers and decomposers, finally returning back to the environment encircling the cycle. The food made by the green plants through the phenomanon of photosynthesis is the ultimate source of food for the entire animal world performing the ways of food-chains and food-webs as trophic levels transferring the energy from one level to the other. The mammals show various adaptations to be well-equipped for a particular environment of the particular habitat having particular set of physical/climatic conditions to live in. Prototherians (Monotremes) is the most primitive mammal laying eggs and having cloaca like reptiles. Metatherians (Marsupials) carry their foetus for a short time and the newly born young ones are partially developed at birth and continue maturing inside the mother's brood-pouch for milking. Eutherians carry foetus till its complete development attached with Placenta and thus also called as placental, means the newly born youngones are developed to the stage that they can continue the maturation process without egg or pouch. Primates are the most evolved and advanced among the placental mammals having highly developed brain (intelligence), opposable thumb and binocular vision. Human-beings, as a primate, is presently the supermost species among the whole animal kingdom having conceptual thought and intelligence ruling the earth planet.

As far as, zoogeographical regions are concerned, the main mammals found in different regions may be summarised as follows:

1) Palaearctic Region : This region extends to the whole of the Europe, China, Japan, North Sahara, Siberia, Mediterranian, Manchuria, Asia, North of Himalaya and North of Arabia. The region is surrounded by sea from three sides viz. West, North, and East, and on the southern side by Sahara and Himalayas. It has continuous connecting link with its two neighbouring regions of Ethiopian and Oriental. The climate is chiefly temperate having arctic tinge in it including both wet forest lands and dry open steppe land, large areas of coniferous forest and some tundra. Thus, great degree of climatic variability is found and variations in fauna are also exhibited as the natural rule.

The important mammalian fauna found in this region are Moles, Shrews, Pandas, Pigs, Rabbits, Squirrels, Dear, Dog, Cat families etc. Yak, Musk Deer, Great Panda, Tibetan Langur, Chinese Water Deer are endemic.

2) Neoarctic Region: It comprises North America above the tropics, New Foundland and Mexican plateau, and Greenland. It is also connected by a very narrow strip with Central America and from all other sides by the sea. The climate is varied and similar to Palaearctic region. It has extensive mountain ranges in the west running from north to south. There are coniferous belt, deciduous forests in eastern part of North America and grasslands in the central part and also the arid zone in the south-west part of North America.

Most commonly found mammals are Rabbits, Shrews, Moles, Squirrels, Beavers, Cat families, Bats, Bears, Deer etc. Flying

Squirrels, Tree Porcupines, Starnosed Moles, Canadian Porcupines, Longlegged Bats, American Badgers are exclusive forms of mammals.

3) **Ethiopian Region:** It includes Africa, South of Sahara, Madagascar and South Arabia. All other sides are surrounded by sea except the land link with northern Palaearctic region. The climate is tropical and due to this there is lush growth of evergreen tropical rain forests.

Most distributed mammals are Bats, Shrews, Rabbits, Squirrels, Dogs, Cats etc. The ethiopian mammals are different from oriental such as Lemurs, Loris, Apes, Elephants, Rhinoceros, etc. Hippopotamus, Giraffes, Rodents, Zebra, Antelopes are exclusive of thie region while Bear, Deer and Sheep are absent here.

4) **Oriental Region:** It covers entire Indian sub-continent, Indo- China, Philippines and South China. The region abounds varied climatic conditions and represented by tropical rain forest in Burma, Indo-China, North-East Asia and Southern part of India. Temperate climate includes Northern part of India.

The chief mammals of this region are Shrews, Rabbits, Squirrels, Dogs, Mustelids, Cat families, Bovids, Civets, Hyaenas, Pigs, Porcupines, Apes, Pangolins, Elephants, Rhinoceros, Old World Monkeys, Bears, Moles and Deer. Gibbons, Tarsiers, Flying Lemur and Tree Shrew are exclusive.

5) **Australian Region:** It contains Australia, New Zealand, Tasmania, New Guinea and other islands. The regions is completely isolated having no link with any other region. Both tropical and temperate climates are found. Northern part of Australia and New Guinea are tropical while

Tasmania is temperate, the interior areas of North Austrailia are arid.

The main mammals are Monotremes and Marsupials, Mice, Australian Dogs, Squirrel etc. Complete absence of higher placental mammals. Marsupials constitute the uniqueness of this region.

6) Neotropical Region: It consists South America, Central America, tropical low land of South Maxico and West Indies. Climatic condition is tropical but the southern part of South America has temperate zone. Due to tropical climate, extensive evergreen forests are found in the Amazon Valley while in Argentina and Saveinna tracts have drier patches and in Western South America sub-desert conditions are found.

Important mammals are Opossum Marsupials, Sloths, Armidallos, New World Monkeys, Rabbits, Deer, Squirrels, New World Porcupines and Rodants. Moles, Hyaenas and Hedgehogs are absent in this region.

As far as biomes/forest types are concerned, the salient mammals found in different biomes may be summarised as follows.

1) The Tropical Rain Forest-Such forests lie between the Tropics of Cancer and Capricorn in five continents from southernmost part of North America into northwestern South America and the entire Amazon basin; in the western half of the equatorial Africa and in eastern Madagascar; and in most of the Indo-Malayan archipelago into northeastern Australia. The forest has characteristic feature like year-round temperature of about 27°C, more than 200 cm of annual rainfall but not less than 12 cm in any month and extremely high humidity. Due to such uniformity of climate, there is year-round growing season of the forest like germination, flowering and fruiting. The decay proceeds so rapidly in such moist forest that humus is completely lacking. Such forest is very important to the life of this earth planet having luxuriant vegetation in comparison to the other biomes supplying maximum oxygen to the planet by the process of photosynthesis.

The main mammalian species found in this forest type are Murine Opossum (*Marmosa sp.*), Water Opossum or Yapok (*Chironectes ninimus*), Haitian Solenodon (*Solenodon paradoxus*), Wrinklefaced Bat (*Centurio senex*), Diskwinged Bat (*Thyroptera tricolor*), Fisherman Bat or Mexican Bulldog Bat (*Noctilio leporinus*), Common Vampire Bat (*Desmodus rotundus*), Mexican Fruit Bat (*Artibeus jamaicensis*), False Vampire Bat (*Vampyrum spectrum*), Golden Lion Marmoset (*Leontideus rosalia*), Spider Monkey (*Ateles sp.*), Capuchin (*Cebus capucinus*), Red Uakari (*Cacajao rubicundus*), Howler Monkey (*Alouatta sp.*), Night Monkey or Douroucouli (*Aotus trivirgatus*), Squirrel Monkey (*Saimiri Sciureus*), Giant Armadillo (*Priodontes giganteus*), Giant Anteater (*Myrmecophaga tridactyla*), Twotoed Sloth (*Choloepus sp.*), Capybara (*Hydrochoerus hydrochaeris*), Prehensiletailed Porcupine (*Coendou prehensilis*), Paca (*Agouti paca*), Jaguar (*Panthera onca*), Tayra (*Eira barbara*), Kinkajou (*Potos flavus*), Coatimundi (*Nasua nasua*), Central American Tapir (*Tapirus bairdi*), Brocket Deer (*Mazama sp.*) Giant African Water Shrew (*Potamogale velox*), Hero Shrew (*Scutisorex congicus*), Old World Leafnosed Bat (*Hipposideros caffer*),Galago or Bush Baby (*Galago senegalensis*), Indri (*Indri indri*), Fattailed Dwarf Lemur (*Cheirogaleus medius*), Ringtailed Lemur (*Lemur catta*), Aye-aye (*Daubentonia madagascariensis*), Colobus Monkey

(*Colobus sp.*), Callared Mangabey (*Cercocebus torquatus*), Gorilla (*Gorilla gorilla*), Mandrill (*Papio sphinx*), Chimpanzee (*Chimpansee troglodytes*), Pangolin (*Manis sp.*), West African Scalytailed Squirrel (*Anomalurops beecrofti*), African Dormouse (*Graphiurus murinus*), Oilpalm Squirrel (*Protoxerus stangeri*), African Palm Civet (*Nandinia binotata*), Golden Cat (*Profelis aurata*), Tree Hyrax (*Dendrohyrax sp.*), Duiker (*Cephalophus sp.*), Bongo (*Taurotragus euryceros*), Giant Forest Hog (*Hylochoerus meinertzhageni*), Okapi (*Okapia johnstoni*), Moon Rat (*Echinosorex gymnurus*), Tree Shrew (*Tupaia sp.*), Colugo or Flying Lemur (*Cynocephalus variegatus*), Rousette Fruit Bat (*Rousettus sp.*), Slow Loris (*Nycticebus coucang*), Mindanao Tarsier (*Tarsius syrichta*), Proboscis Monkey (*Nasalis larvatus*), Crabeating Macaque (*Macaca fascicularis*), Orang-utan (*Pongo pygmaeus*), Lar Gibbon (*Hylobates sp.*), Prevost's Squirrel (*Callosciurus prevosti*), Brushtailed Porcupine (*Atherurus sp.*), Indian Dhole or Red Dog or Wild Dog (*Cuon alpinus*), Malayan Sun Beer (*Helarctos malayanus*), Binturong (*Arctictis binturong*), Bengal Tiger or Indian Tiger (*Panthera tigris tigris*), Muntjac or Barking Deer (*Muntiacus muntjak*), Gaur or Indian Bison (*Bos gaurus*), Duckbilled Platypus (*Ornithorhynchus anatinus*), striped Possum (*Dactylopsila sp.*), Green Ringtail (*Pseudocheirus archeri*), Tasmanian Devil (*Sarcophilus harrisii*), Spotted Cuscus (*Phalanger maculatus*), Tree Kangaroo (*Dendrolagus sp.*) Koala (*Phascolarctos cinereus*), Sugar Glider (*Petaurus breviceps*), Numbat or Marsupial Anteater (*Myrmecobius fasciatus*), Red Flying Fox (*Pteropus scapulatus*).

(2) The Temperate Deciduous Forest- Such forest lie in Central and Western Europe, North America, East Asia, China, Korea and Japan. Rainfall is plentiful (70-150 cm. annually) and there is snowfall during winter. It has luxuriant vegetation and broad leaved tree species are the characteristic of this forest and shedding of leaves takes place in every autumn.

The forest has variety of wonderful mammals namely Opossum (*Didelphis virginiana*), Lesser American short-tailed Shrew (*Cryptotis parva*), Starnosed Mole (*Condylura cristata*), Red Bat (*Lasiurus borealis*), Big Brown Bat (*Eptesicus fuscus*), Keen's Bat (*Myotis keenii*), Eastern Cottontail (*Sylvilagus floridanus*), Woodchuck (*Marmota monax*), Woodland Jumping Mouse (*Napaeozapus insignis*), Southern Flying Squirrel (*Glaucomys volans*), Rice Rat (*Oryzomys palustris*), Eastern Chipmunk (*Tamias striatus*), Cotton Rat (*Sigmodon hispidus*), Musk Rat (*Ondatra zibelhica*), Striped Skunk (*Mephitis mephitis*), River Otter (*Lutra canadensis*), Grey Fox (*Urocyon cinereoargenteus*), Raccoon (*Procyon lotor*), Whitetailed Deer (*Odocoileus virginianus*), Common Shrew (*Sorex araneus*), Hedgehog (*Erinaceus europaeus*), Old World Mole (*Talpa europaea*), Lesser Horseshoe Bat (*Rhinolophus hipposideros*), Pipistrelle (*Pipistrellus pipistrellus*), Longeared Bat (*Plecotus auritus*), Brown Hare (*Lepus capensis*), Old World Rabbit (*Oryctolagus cuniculus*), House Mouse (*Mus musculus*), Norway Rat (*Rattus norvegicus*), Edible Dormouse (*Myoxus glis*), Northern Root Vole or Pine Vole (*Pitymus subterranus*), Old World Wood Mouse or Field Mouse (*Apodemus sp.*), Old World Badger (*Meles meles*), Wild Cat (*Felis silvestris silvestris*),. Pole Cat (*Mustela putorius*), Genet (*Genetta genetta*), Roe Deer (*Capreolus capreolus*), Giant Panda (*Ailuropoda melanoleuca*), Wild Boar (*Sus scrofa*), Chinese Water Deer (*Hydropotes inermis*), Musk Deer (*Moschus chrysogaster/ moschiferus*).

(3) The Coniferous Forest- It is evergreen forest lying northern hemisphere between Tundra and 50° latitude and is the largest forest on earth covering Taiga. It is very cold ranging -30° to -20°C temperature wtih several feet deep snow in maximum period of the year. Rainfall is moderate from 30 to 75 cm annually. Coniferous trees are the characteristic of this forest.

The main mammalian species of this forest are Northern Pika (*Ochotona hyperborea*), Wood Lemming (*Myopus schisticolor*), European Tree Squirrel or Red Squirrel (*Sciurus vulgaris*), Old World Flying Squirrel (*Pteromys volans*), Siberian Chipmunk (*Eutamias sibiricus*), Brown Bear (*Ursus arctos*), Red Fox (*Vulpes vulpes*), Pine Marten (*Martes martes*), European Mink (*Mustela lutreola*), Lynx (*Lynx lynx*), Pygmy Shrew (*Microsorex hoyi*), Varying Hare or Snowshoe Hare (*Lepus americanus*), Aplodontia or Mountain Beaver or Sewellel (*Aplodontia rufa*), North American Red Squirrel (*Tamiasciurus hudsonicus*), Beaver (*Castor canadensis*), Deer Mouse or Whitefooted Mouse (*Peromyscus sp.*), Porcupine (*Erethizon dorsatum*), Black Bear (*Euarctos americanus*), Cougar or Puma or Mountain Lion (*Felis concolor*), Elk or Wapiti (*Cervus canadensis*), Moose (*Alces alces*).

(4) The Tropical Grassland- Actually, Savanna has been named to the largest area of grassland in the world found in Africa lying between Tropic of Capricorn and Tropic of Cancer. Though the grassland is originally implied on a area with a few scattered trees, but now includes also the grasslands having moderately or heavily grown trees. The distinguishing features of such biome is relatively constant and high year-round temperature (21°C) and extremes of drought and wetness following summer and winter. In India, such biome is mostly man-made due to deforestation.

The main mammals found in such biome are Longeared

Elephant Shrew (*Elephantulus sp*), Vervet Monkey (*Cercopithecus aethiops*), Baboon (*Papio sp.*), African Mole Rat (*Tachyoryctes splendens*), Zebra Mouse or Striped Grass Mouse (Lemniscomys sp.), Cane Rat (*Thryonomys sp.*), Ratel or Honey Badger (*Mellivora capensis*), African Wild Dog or Hunting Dog (*Lycaon pictus*), Spotted Hyaena (*Crocuta crocuta*), Leopard or Panther (*Panthera pardus*), Lion (*Panthera leo*), Cheetah (*Acinonyx jubatus*), African Elephant (*Loxodonta africana*), Aardvark (*Orycteropus afer*), Rock Hyrax (*Heterohyrax sp*). Grant's Zebra (*Equus burchelli*), Black Rhinoceros (*Diceros bicornis*), Wart Hog (*Phacochoerus aethiopicus*), Giraffe (*Giraffa camelopardalis*), Hippopotamus (*Hippopotamus amphibius*), African Buffalo (*Syncerus caffer*), Grant's Gazelle (*Gazella granti*), Dik-dik (*Madoqua sp.*), Hartebeest (*Alcelaphus buselaphus*), Sable Antelope (*Hippotragus niger*), Gerenuk (*Litocranius walleri*), Klipspringer (*Oreotragus oreotragus*.), Blue Wildebeest (*Connochaetes taurinus*), Eland (*Taurotragus oryx*), Spiny Anteater or Echidna (*Tachyglossus aculeatus*), Red Kangaroo (*Macropus rufus*), Hairynosed Wombat (*Lasiorhinus sp.*), Rufous Rat-Kangaroo (*Aepyprymnus rufescens*), Ghost Bat (*Macroderma gigas*), Spectacled Hare-Wallaby (*Lagorchestes conspicillatus*), Longhaired Rat (*Rattus villosissimus*), Ninebanded Armadillo (*Dasypus novemcinctus*), Maned Wolf (*Chrysocyon brachyurus*), Entellus Langur (*Presbytis entellus*), Fourhorned Antelope (*Tetracerus quadricornis*), Cheetal or Spotted Dear (*Axis axis*), Blackbuck (*Antilope cervicapra*).

(5) The Temperate Grasslands- It lies in the middle latitudes of the northen hemisphere and lower latitudes of the southern. Such biome is found in every continent of the world and called as steppe, prairie or plains, pampas in different places. The rainfall is not very low and drought persists for the most part of the year and temperature varies as per the season from about 35ºC to -15ºC.

The prevailing mammalian species found in this biome are Steppe Lemming (*Lagurus lagurus*), Spottted Souslik (*Citellus suslicus*), Common Hamster (*Cricetus cricetus*), Mole-vole (*Ellobius talpinus*), Birch Mouse (*Sicista subtilis*), Marbled Polecat (*Vormela peregusna*), Saiga Antelope (*Saiga tatarica*), Blacktailed Prairie Dog (*Cynomys ludovicianus*), American Harvest Mouse (*Reithrodontomys sp.*), Pocket Gopher (*Geomys sp.*), Prairie vole (*Microtus ochrogaster*), Coyote (*Canis latrans*), Spotted Skunk (*Spilogale putorius*), Pronghorn (*Antilocapra americana*), Bison (*Bison bison*), Plains Viscacha (*Lagostomus maximus*), Cavy or Guinea Pig (*Cavia sp.*), Tuco-tuco (*Ctenomys sp.*), Pampas Fox (*Dusicyon gymnocercus*), Vicuna (*Vicugna vicugna*).

(6) The Desert- In deserts; lack of water, much fluctuation in daily temperature (55ºC to 15ºC) and widely distributed plants are the characteristic features and roughly lie along Tropics of Cancer and Capricorn. The plants as well as animals have remarkable adaptations living in such area specially to conserve water and tolerate heat.

The salient mammals of this biome are Desert Hedgehog (*Hemiechinus sp.*), Desert Jerboa (*Jaculus jaculus*), Spiny Mouse (*Acomys cahirinus*), Springhare (*Pedetes capensis*), Fennec (*Fennecus zerda*), Sand-dune Cat (*Felis margarita*), Dromedary (*Camelus dromedarius*), Addax (*Addax nasomaculatus*), Aoudad or Barbary Sheep (*Ammotragus lervia*), Dorcas Gazelle (*Gazella dorcas*), Marsupial Mole or Pouched Mole (*Notoryctes typhlops*), Euro or Wallaroo or Hill Kangaroo (*Macropus robustus*), Rabbiteared Bandicoot or Bilby (*Thylacomys sp.*), Rock Wallaby (*Petrogale penicillata*), Dingo

(*Canis dingo*), Australian Hopping Mouse (*Notomys alexis*), Mongolian Gerbil (*Meriones unguiculatus*), Asiatic Jackal (*Canis aureus*), Mongoose (*Herpestes sp.*), Kulan or Mongolian Wild Ass (*Equus hemionus hemionus*), Goitered Gazelle (*Gazella subgutturosa*), Freetailed Bat (*Tadarida brasiliensis*), Blacktailed Jack Rabbit (*Lepus californicus*), Desert Wood Rat (*Neotoma lepida*), Antelope Ground Squirrel (*Ammospermophilus leucurus*), Pocket Mouse (*Perognathus penicillatus*), Javelina or Collared Peccary (*Tayassu tajacu*), Mara or Patagonian Cavy or Patagonian Hare (*Dolichotis sp.*), Peludo (*Chaetophractus sp.*), Pichi (*Zaedyus pichiy*), Pink Fairy Armadillo (*Chlamyphorus truncatus*), Guanaco (*Lama guanacoe*).

(7) The Tundra-Tundra means barren ground without trees which cannot grow due to very low temperature. It lies in North Pole continuously between icy Arctic Ocean and the tree line. The temperature varies from 15°C to -50°C and light intensity is also very low. Annual rainfall is only upto 20 cm and condition is like desert. Hence, very limited variety of low growing vegetation are found in this biome. The animals are highly specialized in adaptation to suit in such environment.

The main mammals found in this biome are Arctic Shrew/ Siberian Shrew / Masked Shrew (*Sorex sp.*), Arctic Hare (*Lepus arcticus*), Arctic Ground Squirrel or Arctic Souslik (*Spermophilus undulatus*), Tundra Redback Vole (*Clethrionomys sp.*) Norway Lemming (*Lemmus lemmus*), Timber Wolf or Grey Wolf (*Canis lupus*), Arctic Fox (*Alopex lagopus*), Wolverine or Glutton (*Gulo gulo*), Stoat or Ermine (*Mustela erminea*), Polar Bear (*Thalarctos maritimus*), Caribou or Reindeer (*Rangifer tarandus*), Musk Ox (*Ovibos moschatus*), Alpine Marmot (*Marmota marmota*), Mountain Goat

(*Oreamnos americanus*), Ibex (*Capra ibex*), Bighorn Sheep (*Ovis canadensis*), Chamois (*Rupicapra rupicapra*).

(8) The Ocean- The marine/aquatic animals are highly adapted and specialized to suit in such type of biome.

The major mammalian species found here are Minke Whale (*Balaenoptera acutorostrata*), California Grey Whale (*Eschrichtius robustus*), Black Right Whale (*Eubalaena glacialis*), Sperm Whale or Cachalot (*Physeter catodon*), Narwhal (*Monodon monoceros*), Killer Whale (*Orcinus orca*), Freshwater Dolphin (*Inia geoffensis* etc.), Bottlenosed Dolphin (*Tursiops truncatus*), Harbor Porpoise (*Phocoena phocoena*), Spinning Dolphin (*Stenella longirostris*), Sea Otter (*Enhydra lutris*), Harbor Seal (*Phoca vitulina*), Elephant Seal (*Mirounga sp.*) Northern Fur Seal (*Callorhinus ursinus*), California Sea Lion (*Zalophus californianus*), Walrus (*Odobenus rosmarus*), Dugong (*Dugong sp.*), Manatee (*Trichechus sp.*).

In these days, the main agency causing changes and elimination of numerous animal forms, is the man because man sweeps away forests, rivers etc. and manipulate the wildlife habitats as per his own desires and benefits washing out existing races/species of animals. Though man is a destructive agent, he may be also protecter and preserver of wild creatures from the destructive effects of his own work done. Various factors, as a result of human activities, are threatening the wildlife. Man must save the wild creatures and natural resources with their uses judiciously to save the environment and ultimately human-race. There is great need of adequate measures to be taken with scientific planning to preserve, protect and propagate wildlife to avoid their further depletion and destruction. In brief, it can be said that without the existence of wildlife, the existence and survival of human-race is at stake.

Chapter **4**

Need of Wildlife Conservation and Management

In previous chapters, the necessity of wildlife conservation has been discussed which aims the wildlife to be in peak status in nature to maintain natural-balance and not with the objective to get benefit. Now question arises, how to conserve and propagate them to get benefit from them alongwith conservation. For the purposes, wildlife management comes into light to fulfil the aims and objectives which includes efficient utilization of the natural resources to the maximum human benefit through the process of scientific studies of the population of wild animals and their habitat pattern alongwith conservation. We can say that wildlife management is the judicious use of wildlife resource towards the attainment of scientific, ecological, economical, ethical, aesthetic and recreational objectives for the benefit of human-beings and for the improvement of nature upon which all the components of ecosystem depend. It also includes planning and studying of habitat and behaviours of wild animal's population. Thus, wildlife management is the science and art of manipulation of structure, dynamics and relations of the wild populations, their habitat and the concerned people in order to achieve specific human goals by means of wildlife resource. In wildlife management, there is conservation of wildlife but alongwith this they are also managed in such a way that they can meet the specific objectives of human-beings. According to R.H. Giles, "Wildlife management is the science and art of changing the characteristics and interactions of habitats, wild populations, and such in order to achieve specific human goals by means of wildlife resource. These goals may frequently be sport-recreation, but may also include or be restricted to aesthetic, economic and ecological goals. Those working in the area of wildlife management are ultimately involved in the manipulation of the complex man-land-animal triad". Further, he also expanded Leopold's definition as "Wildlife management is the science and art of changing the characteristics and interactions of habitats, wild animal population, and men is order to achieve specific human goals by means of wildlife resource". Since wildlife is a renewable natural resource as well as an ecologic science, it forms an integral part of the land and involves a type of land-use including other living things that co-inhabit the same basic resources of soil, water, vegetation and atmosphere. Observing the definition of Giles, wildlife management is the science as well as art. It is the science in studying long time detailed research and observation of life and ecology of wildlife of get scientific records and to formulate principles to evolve system of management to achieve specific goal. Based on these knowledge, the wildlife management starts. Different wildlife managers at different places applying their capacity of art can get different types of results. The definition also says about specific goals of human beings in the wildlife management plan and, therefore, planning of management should be planned in such a way that the specific goal may be achieved. Besides these, there is also two important aspects of definition such as habitat of wildlife and related people.

Hence, the main objective of wildlife management is to establish favourable balance among these three aspects viz. wildlife, habitat and people by manipulating their structure, dynamics and relations. Among these aspects; wildlife population itself, its habitat which includes food, water and shelter, and related people who remain in and around the habitats are under considerations. Appropriate manipulation is essential for successful management of wildlife among all these aspects for the improvement in wildlife status and its enhancement so that specific goal may be achieved.

It is recognized world over that biological diversity is an insurance for food and ecological security. But it is threatened by encroachment and alteration on natural ecosystems by the activities of the ever growing human population. The creation of new species and elimination of a few others are the results of organic evolution. Extinction of a species is also a part of the natural process. But with the gradual emergence of human beings as a major evolutionary force, people have been increasingly exploiting the wildlife rather conserving them. The rate of decline has been particularly rapid in the about last one hundred years without any simultaneous renewal. It is estimated that about 25,000 plant species and 1,000 vertebrate species and subspecies are threatened and on the verge of extinction all over the world. The above figures are excluding invertebrates and other forms of life which are also passing through vulnerable stage. It is supposed that at least 10 per cent of the living species are in danger. As stated earlier the most serious threat to the wildlife comes from habitat destruction and its shrinkage. Habitats, which protect wildlife are being converted to human settlements, harbours, dams, reservoirs, croplands, grazing grounds, plantations, mining sites etc. The introduction of exotic species, over-exploitation and international trade in increasingly scarce commodities of wild origin, mainly from developing countries, are other causes of destruction and depletion of many species. That's why, the rare and threatened species of wild animals and plants have been categorized for conservation purposes by the International Union of Conservation of Nature and Natural Resources (IUCN) which is now called WCU (World Conservation Union). Majorly, the following categories have been identified.

(i) Endangered (E) - These are the species whose numbers have been reduced to a critical level or whose habitats have been so drastically reduced that they are deemed to be in immediate damager of extinction.

(ii) Vulnerable (V) - These are species whose population have been seriously depleted and whose ultimate security is not assured and also those whose population are still abundant, but are under threat throughout their range.

(iii) Rare (R) - These are species with small populations in the world. These are not at present endangered and vulnerable but are at risk.

(iv) Threatened (T) - The term "threatened" is used in the context of conservation of the species which are in any one of the above three categories viz. E, V or R.

The IUCN maintains a "red database" at the World Conservation Monitoring Centre (WCMC). From time to time, this database is translated into popular document and published as Red List or Red Data Book of species that are facing the risk of extinction. In India, Botanical Survey of India (BSI) published a Red Book for endangered plant species which should be provided with conservation. There are mainly three specific objectives of conservation of biodiversity such as -

(a) To maintain essential ecological process and life-supporting systems (air, water and soil).

(b) To preserve the diversity of species or the range of genetic material of world's organisms.

(c) To ensure a continuous use of speices, in fact ecosystem, that support rural communities and urban industries.

Thus, the conservation of wildlife has broad objective, not only concerned with biotic (plants, animals and microorganisms) but also with abiotic factors. Therefore, conservation of biodiversity is a complex operation, which is specifically concerned with plants, animals and microorganisms and with these non living elements of the environment on which they depend. Scientists representing 100 countries of the world have evolved a comprehensive World Conservation Strategy for judicious use of resources. Some of the important steps among those are -

- Preservation of species which have been marked endangered.

- Sound planning and management of land and water uses. The wild life should be protected both in their natural habitats (*in situ*) and in zoos and botanical gardens (*ex situ*).

- Preservation of as many varieties as possible of food crops, forage plants, timber trees, livestocks, animals for aquaculture and their wild relative and microbes. Priority should be given to those varieties that are most threatened and most needed for national and international breeding programme.

- Each country should identify the habitats of wild relatives of the economically valuable and useful plants and animals and ensure their preservation in Protected Areas.
- Safefuarding of the critical habitats (the feeding, breeding, nursery and resting areas) of the species.
- Establishing a network of Protected Areas for migratory or wide ranging animals to preserve the habitat of the species.
- If a species migrates or ranges from one national jurisdiction to another, bilateral or multilateral agreements should be made to set up the required network. Exploitation of the species and pollution of the environment along the migration routes should be regulated.
- Unique ecosystem should be protected as a matter of priority. Only those uses which are compatible, with their preservation, should be permitted.
- The productive capacities of exploited species and ecosystems have to be determined and it has to be ensured that utilization does not exceed those capacities.
- International trade in wild plants and animals has to be regulated to appropriate legislative and administrative measures.

Methods of conservation of faunal and floral species are broadly classified into two methods which are *in situ* conservation is the most appropriate method. This approach includes protection of total ecosystems through a network of protected Areas. The common natural habitats (Protected

Areas) that have been set for *in situ* conservation of wildlife include national parks, sanctuaries, biosphere reserves, several wetlands, mangroves, coral reefs, sacred groves and lakes. *Ex situ* conservation of threatened animal species in botanical species in the form of seeds in Seed Banks etc. by means of tissue-culture techniques. Individual of the species are maintained in artificial conditions under human supervision. These methods include maintaining Gene Banks, Pollen Preservation and the most useful is the Cryopreservation by which tissue culture and germ plasm conservation are made. Thus, methods of biodiversity conservation may be presented as below -

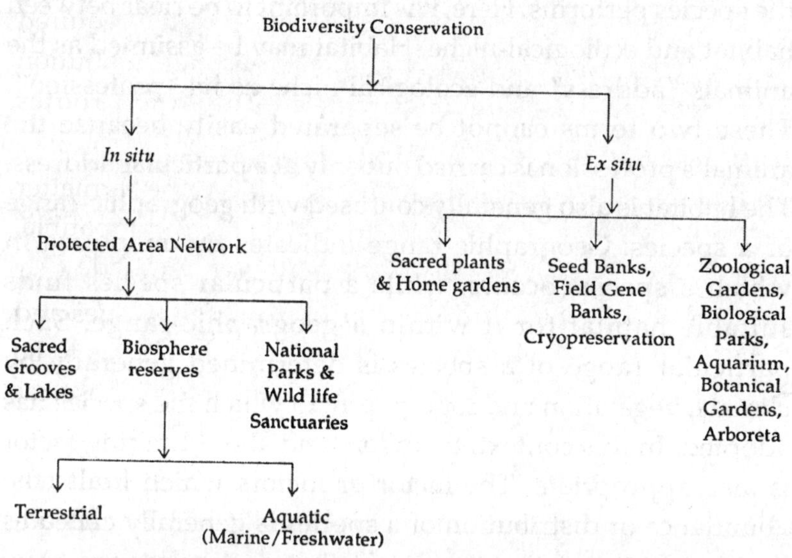

Fig. Methods of Biodiversity conservation

If we want to maintain or restore wild animals, we must leave for them a place to live which is habitat (a place and an environment suited to a particular speices). Habitat management or manipulation to benefit wildlife can mean anything from complete protection of remote areas to drastic disturbance of vegetation to create those successional stages favourable to certain species. In all habitats there is a limit to the number of animals of any one species that can be supported. That limit is known as carrying-capacity of that habitat. Behind determining the carrying-capacity, certain factors are involved like right kind of food and availability of its quality; presence of water for most of the animals; right kind of soil for required species; necessary topography such as mountains, plains, lakes, streams; cover and shelter which are arrangements of land and vegetation suited to nesting, resting, hiding, flying; and all the various activities which the species performs. Here, it is important to be clear between habitat and ecological-niche. Habitat may be assumed as the animals "address" and ecological-niche as its "profession". These two terms cannot be separated easily because the animal's profession is carried out only at a particular address. The habitat is also generally confused with geographic-range of a species. Geographic range indicates the map area in which a species occurs, while a particular species finds suitable habitat for it within a geographic-range. Such particular range of a species is determined generally by climate, vegetation and topography to which the species has adopted. In this context, to understand about limiting factor is also appropriate. The factor or factors which limits the abundance or distribution of a species is generally called as limiting factor of that species in that particular area. Any organism requires a complex of environmental conditions and has a range of tolerance to any one of them. Any condition that surpasses the limits of tolerance for that organism becomes a limiting factor for it, Sheldford postulated the theory known as Law of Tolerance stating that all environmental factors have a tolerable limit, the critical minimum and critical-maximum. The range between these two is called limit of Tolerance. If for a particular species, the tolerance exceeds its limit, the species will disappear from that particular area as long as such condition exists. Thus, the degree of completition, co-operation and other relations between the animals depend upon a number of factors, and the complexity of these factors in space and time indicates the dynamic character of wildlife ecology. Species whose population is dwindling may ultimately reach an extinction-threshold, where a minimum number is required for survival which is biological minimum number. If this minimum number decreases below this extinction-threshold, the rebuilding of the species is impossible and extinction of the species results which is known as critical-limit for that particular species. Generally, it is difficult to identify a single limiting factor because presence and absence of an organism or a group of organisms in an ecosystem depends upon a complex of factors and entire complex of conditions involved. Therefore, the approach towards the limiting factor should cover all the aspects of ecosystem and a single species approach may not be helpful in proper understanding of the various interactions in population, factors, habitat etc. From wildlife management point of view, we should follow wholestic concept of the ecosystem.

In ancient years, the wildlife in India were found sufficiently, but as described in previous chapters, due to tremendous growth in human population followed by poverty and unemployment, deforestation started for converting forest land into agricultural purposes and subsequently the habitat of wildlife started shrinking and shrinking and their population depleted and is still depleting. The period of

Second World War was the most devastating period for wildlife as the animals were killed mercilessly wherever militaries got shelter. Main reasons causing depletion in wildlife population may be said as follows:

- Conversion of forests into agricultural fields.
- In ancient years, hunting was done mercilessly, recklessly, wontonly and unscientifically.
- Construction of forest roads, dams, etc.
- Establishment of industries in forest areas.
- Occurrence of mines etc.
- Use of firearms in hunting and hunting were not done selflessly but to get cheap money by greedy people and so on.
- Increase in livestock and grazing by them in forest areas resulting loss in food and shelter of wild animals alongwith spreading infection of diseases in wild animals.
- Selfishness and greediness in certain people to earn money through wild animals and its products.
- Pollution of environment, rivers, water reservoirs and ocean by insecticides, fertilizers, polluted gas and water from industries as by-products.
- Tremendous growth in human population.
- Lack of awareness among masses towards importance of wildlife and forest.
- Liting of fire by the local people inside the forests.
- Poverty and unemployment and lack of alternative source of earning by the local people living in and around the habitats of wildlife.

The above factors not only depleted number of wild animals but some of them also became extinct, some are threatened/ endangered and some are on the verge of extinction. They all together have come to the alarming stage and the benefit meeting by them in respect of revenue is presently negligible. That's why, the hunting or doing any harm to the wild animals is now totally banned and treated as an offence, by law in our country. Hence, wildlife management is the techniques related to wildlife conservation through which wild animals could be helped propagate as the renewable natural resource and before choosing the management techniques, it is essential to keep in mind the prime objectives of management as well as target species. The planning of management in general may be categorized in the following steps:-

i) Census :- Before moving forward towards management, it is necessary to find out the present status of the wild animal species in particular habitat regarding its present number, sex-ratio and age-ratio. For the purpose, wildlife census is essential. To access the number of the species population available in the habitat is very important so that further studies, research and appropriate strategies may be planned on that very basis and, if necessary, to remove decimating factor acting as causal agent for the species concerned so that the population may be brought to the carrying-capacity or optimum density or subsistence density or beyond that as per desire to get revenue also. Hence, without getting the above mentioned knowledge, it is impossible to decide the management technique to be applied for obtaining desired objectives.

(ii) Productivity:- The measurement of productivity of the species is determined to compare its standard productivity to find out the present situation as whether its productivity is normal or below or above the standard level. For the purpose; natality rate, mortality rate, environmental resistance, prey and predator relationship, carrying capacity, hunting and poaching, intra and interspecific behavioural aspect, availability of food, water and shelter, availability of core and buffer food species, edge effect, decimating factors etc. are thoroughly studied to access the present status of productivity of the species particularly the target species. On the basis of the studies, appropriate measures are applied accordingly in respect of habitat management/ manipulation and population management /manipulation and so on.

iii) Control measures:- From management point of view, it is necessary to find out the factor which is hampering the growth etc. of the population of wild animal species. Hence, to apply control measures against such factor and get remedy is an important aspect of wildlife management so that the population may reach to the desired level giving progressive result.

iv) Treatment:- Application of controlling measure against the limiting factor to overcome the problem, is the treatment. Such factor of damaging may be decimating factor or the scarcity of food, water or shelter. Therefore, after diagnosis of such causal factor and treatment of control measure for that is an important tool in the field of wildlife management.

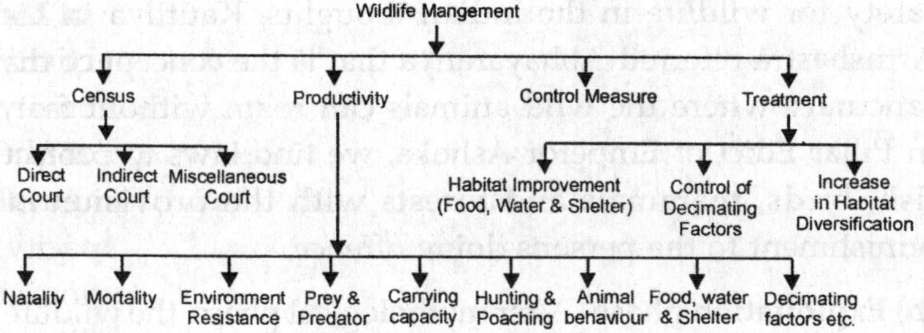

Fig. General Steps of Wildlife Management

As far as history of wildlife conservation or management is concerned, it may be divided into three following phases in India-

(a) Mythological Phase:- It is the period in which wild animals were getting priority of protection through religious sentiment. There are so many legends and preaches communicating the message of saving and protecting wild animals. Saints always taught the lession of conserving and protecting wild animals. There are so many stories in this regard also. King Pandu in Mahabharata was cursed by the hind deer for shooting her stag in mating. Rama was helped by Hanuman against Ravana. The eight celestial points of the compass being supposed to be guarded by India's elephant. Lion is one of the many incarnations of God Vishnu, tiger has place being mentioned in the later Vedic texts, mongoose noticed in Mahabharata as a teacher of wisdom to King Yudhistir, deer is always associated with God Brahma, cobra is the constant companion of God Mahadeva and the wild boar is referred to as "Boar & Heaven". About thirty different mammals are mentioned by name in Samhitas (the four principal Vedas). It is interesting to know the world that the earliest measures taken for the protection of animals come from India. All these protective measures have secured safety for wildlife in the Indian thoughts. Kautilya in his Arthshastra referred Abhayaranya that is the concept of the sanctuary where the wild animals can roam without fear. In Pillar Edict of Emperor Ashoka, we find laws to protect fish, birds, mammals and forests with the provision of punishment to the persons doing offence.

(b) Exploitation phase- After mythological phase, the wildlife faced ever-increasing pressure and called as exploitation phase. Moghuls hunted wild animals including birds a lot, though they were having keen interest in nature and management was concentrated for game. In British period, hunting was going on for the pleasure of kings and princes. This era of exploitation continued with increasing India's population and simultaneously forest land was encroached and cleared for agricultural purposes. Even after independence, pressure on forest and wild animals continued. It can be said that depletion in wildlife started in the middle of 19th century and the Second World War was the most dangerous and devastating period. However, British people realized the importance of wildlife and enforced various Acts to save them.

(c) Conservation Phase- This phase for India's wild animals came since independence with general consciousness as a period of conservation and propagation of wild animals followed by world movement to conserve natural resources wisely and scientifically keeping balanced relationship with the natural heritage to get benefits in perpetuity. For the purpose, IUCN (International Union for Conservation of Nature & Natural Resources), IBWL (Indian Board for Wildlife), CITES (Convention on International Trade in Endangered Species of Wild Fauna and Flora), WWF

(Worldwide Fund for Nature), BNHS (Bombay Natural History Society) etc. alongwith various NGOs, came into picture with salient objectives aiming conservation and propagation of wildlife to be managed judiciously and scientifically so that their utilization and benefits may be taken on sustained basis in perpetuity from generation after generation maintaining natural-balance. The Wild Life (Protection) Act, 1972 in India is the primary legal control all over the country. Creation of sanctuaries, national parks, etc. are the output of this Act and it is also amended time to time as per the necessity. Presently, hunting or harming any wild animal is totally banned and treated as an offence as per 1991 amendment of the Act. In addition, many projects have been set up to conserve and propagate the threatened species in a nice and proper way.

For effective conservation of wild animals, the management of three fundamental needs such as food, water and shelter must be fulfilled in proper way to achieve the goal. For this, it is essential to manage/manipulate population of wild animals and their habitats to get improvement upto desired level. In respect of population management, different aspects like census to know the status of the species, inter and intraspecific relationship, prey and predator relationship, population stability /structure, introduction for population stability, growth-forms, management of vermin, fire management etc. are studied thoroughly to be acquainted with the real situation. Regarding habitat management, the areas such as food, water and shelter are studied thoroughly to find out the availability of food materials, waterholes and shelter for the species. After gaining thorough knowledge of the above aspects regarding population and habitat, the further strategies are planned to move ahead towards the management to improve the situation, if required. If the position of the species is below carrying-capacity, the management and manipulation is required in the habitat by creating sufficient facilities of the basic needs by improving natural availability as well as artificially by applying scientific management techniques. If the position is above the carrying-capacity, exploitation of the concerned species in scientific way should be carried out, or if possible, carrying-capacity of the habitat may be increased to support the population. Any way, the objective should be first to reach the population as per the carrying-capacity of the habitat and then to bring them to the stage of subsistence-density and beyond that to get biological-surplus or shootable-surplus to find revenue from them. Hence, it is clear that if the population-density of a particular habitat is less than its carrying-capacity, there will be growth in population raising productivity getting food, water and shelter as basic needs in sufficient quantity. Such growth will continue upto the biotic-potential of the species. But when condition goes beyond this level, the habitat will be unable to sustain the unlimited numbers of the individuals of the population and decimating factors will start to act against its growth and biotic-potential resulting in increase in its mortality-rate and in such stage environmental-resistance also minimizes its natality-rate. In this way, biotic-potential acts in the direction of the growth of the population while decimating factors and environmental resistance act in the direction of its death. In the interactions of these factors, when there is a stage of balance, it is called as population-stability; but when there is imbalance among these factors, gain or loss in its numbers is found in accordance with the situation. When biotic-potential of the species is more than that of the environmental-resistance, there will be growth in the population and vice versa. The studies and findings of all the above facts and factors must be very carefully and thoroughly considered otherwise, management plan will be not only unsuccessful but also dangerous and disastrous resulting in adverse effects in the ecosystem and ultimately to the mankind. In the above context the people, living in and around the habitats, should also be managed in the sense of awareness of protection and conservation of the wild animals to achieve the goal. It is the demand of the time that consciousness must be created in their minds about the importance of wildlife as well as need of their conservation and propagation. Without support and participation of the public, particularly local people, fulfilment of the objectives of the plan cannot be achieved up to mark. Hence, awareness and provision of alternative earning engagement to such people is must and should be taken as a movement and challenge.

Overall, to uplift the socio-economic condition and propagation of wildlife, land-use planning must be adopted and implemented wherever required to mitigate the problems of overgrowing human population, poverty and unemployment because the land and the natural resources are limited but the numbers of mouths to feed are going up and up. Under such circumstances, to protect and propagate wildlife is really a difficult task and great challenge. Therefore, concept of multiple-use of land, which can solve the problem upto a large extent, must be followed. Developed countries have already taken steps in this direction and wildlife is viewed as land-use. A piece of land to be managed should be judged by the team of experts of various fields like agriculture, veterinary, forestry, wildlife, fishery, watershed management, soil conservation etc. to be interlinked and suggesting very honestly the proper utility and suitability of the particular piece of land so that each and every piece of land may be utilized in proper way providing maximum productivity avoiding future complications and anomalies, and getting balance in every walk of human life. The areas specially degraded lands, nallas etc. unsuitable for agricultural crops should be managed in operational plan in such a way that it may suit for certain suitable wild animals and birds providing revenue and recreation alongwith their propagation. In our country, there is sufficient chance to link wildlife with land-use planning with other land uses on the basis of multiple land-use concept by understanding wildlife as an important land-use for nature, environment, eco-balance and ultimately human-life. It involves a challenging task of wildlife resource and its integration with economics of the basic planning objectives. This prospective should form a part of our overall developmental strategy to save and propagate our remaining national valuable wildlife heritage.

Chapter 5

Man and Wild Animal Relationship

Mammals, a class to which man himself belongs, unquestoinably and undoubtedly are the highest animals in evolutionary trend due to having superior mental power. Man is the superior most and his superior brain made him mastery over the forces of environment/nature. Today man is the ruler of the earth having supreme power of intelligence enabling him to capture earth, seas, sky etc. and to spread all over the world. Since beginning of human civilization and culture, the man has close relationship with wild animals for various uses and purposes living harmoniously and peacefully. The domestic and pet animals are the salient examples of such relationship. But in span of time being more and more desirous and greedy and growing towards modernisation, the man started to exploit the wild animals mercilessly in unscientific manner resulting today in natural imbalance depleting and depleting wildlife population bringing at alarming stage. The situation is that yesterday we were noising but today we are crying for their protection and propagation. It is the demand of the hour to understand the roles of wild animals played towards natural-balance and survival of mankind. The relationship between man and wild animals is eternal and inevitable. It should be always friendly, lovely and balancing. The relation of man with certain wild animals, as examples, are described below-

Monkeys and Man:

Monkeys belong to order Primate of class Mammalia and they are successfully adapting themselves to human company being social animal. Some men, called as Madari, make them pet with special training of dancing and other activities to exhibit show to the public and earning money in most parts of the country. Such show is very attractive and interesting specially to the children (presently, it is banned in our country by law to make wild animals as pet or other activities). Troops of monkeys/macaques and langurs invade towns and villages etc. and even enter houses. Its ways and habits of life is influenced by the association with man and also show social life when food is provided by man. Monkeys are hunted for their fur and flesh is eaten by some forest tribes of the country. We have known about R^h factor in human blood and likewise chimpanzee helped us in conducting sereological protein test. They are also used in testing newly invented medicines to be used further for man's application. Similarly many such other scientific achievements are related with monkeys which are advancement in our modern civilization in the field of science.

Felidaeans and Man:

Family Felidae under class Mammalia includes tiger, lion, leopard, cats etc. They have close association with man. From time immemorial, animals of cat family (Felidae) have impressed the man for their beautiful forms, hides etc. The great and majestic carnivores are subject of worship, legend, folk-lore, romance, symbol of bravery like lion and tiger etc. Many of them are of medicinal value and the products derived from them are of great economical value. Keeping beautiful fur of certain animals like tiger, lion panther etc. is the symbol of status (now it is totally banned in India by law to hunt any wild animals and treated as an offence). The knowledge of true life, uses and benefits of these animals related to man by studying many factors influenced by them. We have to learn still much about them in our interest.

Mongooses and Man:

Mongooses chiefly feeding on rats, birds, reptiles, frog, insects, crabs, scorpions etc. but are omnivorous and play great role in food-chain balancing the nature. They prey on snakes usually venomous species like cobra is of much interest. It is less sensitive to the venom of snakes and is able to withstand it. The fight between mongoose and snake is very peculiar and gives much pleasure to the spectators. It is also tamed by man particularly to be protected from poisonous snakes. It shows social behaviour with the man. Some people, called as "madari" make them as pet for the purpose of earning by exhibiting its activities as the public shows, however, presently banned by law in our country. Though mongooses damage poultry and crops, they do more benefits than harms by destroying venomous snakes, rats, mice etc. It rapidly rids a house of snakes, rates, mice, scorpions and insects. Its much utility to man is recognised from the ancient times.

Hyaena and Man:

Hyaena is chiefly scavenger in habit feeding on dead and dying animals cleaning the environment and making it hygienic which is useful to man. It provides us pollution-free atmosphere to live in. It also acts as natural-regulator feeding on weak animals when they lack power of resistance. It is also predator hunting sheep, goat, calf, dog etc. and even human child. Its tongue and fat are of medicinal value.

Canadaeans and Man:

Family Canidae of class Mammalia includes dogs, wolves, jackals and foxes. Dogs are acting as man's companion and are pet since the dawn of human civilization. They act as true friend and faithful guard of its master. Though the animals of this family are primarily carnivorous but occasionally take vegetarian food also. They attack sometimes poultry, lamb and goat, and occasionally human child particularly by wolf. They are also carrier of rabies, though it is believed that this disease has been transmitted by the domestic dogs. Dogs have great smelling and sense power and used in catching miscreants by police and defence departments by giving special training. They are also used in hunting to follow and capture the target animal. Primarily, jackal and wolf live on carrion and act as scarvenger cleaning the environment and thus benefiting us a lot. These animals, specially wild dogs, wolves and foxes play important role in serving man indirectly by keeping down the numbers of animals damaging crops. Wild dogs prey pigs which are destructive to crops and likewise foxes prey rodents and small vermin species. In this way, they repay us more than they may do damage.

Bears and Man:

Bears belong to family Ursidae under class Mammalia and has close association with man since the remote time. They are dangerous to man as they do furious attack to man killing him in self-defence, specially by brown bear and black bear, and also damage cattle by killing them being carnivorous in nature. However, the bear, particularly sloth bear, is made captive and trained by certain people, called as Madari, to earn money by exhibiting show to the public entertaining various interesting activities.

Bats and Man:

Bats that belong to order Chiroptera under class Mammalia are true flying mammal and influence us in many ways. They are mainly insect and fruit eaters living near human surroundings and houses. By destroying insect pests, they play beneficial role in human economy. Though, the fruit bats do harm to our economy by eating the fruits but they also spread the seeds of plants and thus help in plant propagation on large scale. They are also of scientific value for us giving inspiration in the field of radar and ultrasonic discoveries and so on.

Rodents and Man:

Rodents comprising squirrels, marmots, rats, mice, porcupine etc. are under order Rodentia of class Mammalia. They are small mammals and supposed to be the largest group among mammals both in number and species living in diversified modes of life. They are chiefly herbivorous and play important role in balancing food-chain of the nature as well as economy by controlling plant life (autotrophs) in the ecosystem providing food as prey to their predators (carnivores). However, rats and mice cause great damage to the agricultural crops both standing as well as stored and give economical loss to man. They are also carriers of deadly diseases like plague etc. But overall view of rodents can be understood in maintenance of food-chain and eco-balance. Order Lagomorpha including hares and rabbits also play very important role in natural-balance as herbivorous animals as stated above.

Elephants and Man:

The elephants which belong to order Proboscidea under class Mammalia are the largest terrestrial animal in the world. It has very close association with man since the beginning of our civilization. They are tamed as well as trained and used as carrier of both man and heavy materials as a means of transport and riding even in war in the past. The time when there was no such advancement in the field of automobile, elephants were the main source of travelling and load carrier including battle field and as a symbol of status by keeping them. Their tusks are of great economic value (now-a-days, its use is banned by law in our country) being used in various purposes. In Hindu mythology, they are regarded and worshipped as "Ganesha" the son of God Shiva. Presently, there is man-elephant (wild elephant) conflict due to damage made by the elephants by taking lives of man and damaging crops, but it is because of mainly habitat destruction done by man himself and requires proper management of its habitat by removing anomolies in this respect to get appropriate balance.

Rhinoceros and Man:

Rhinoceros is placed under order Ungulata of class Mammalia and is of great value specially its horn in the field of medicine. Many belief are connected with this animal. Its blood, flesh and horns are used by certain people for the purpose of worships. The urine is supposed to be antiseptic and is hung in a vessel at the entrance of house to remove ghosts, evil spirits, diseases in some countries particularly in Nepal, Burma and China. Apart from these, the animal being herbivorous in nature play role in natural-balance of the habitat.

Ungalates and Man:

Order Ungulata of class Mammalia comprises two suborders viz. Artiodactyla (even-toed ungulates) consisting hippopotamus, bears, pigs, giraffe, oxen (gaur, buffalo, yak etc), sheeps, goats, antelopes & gazelles (nilgai, blackbuck, chowsingha, chinkara etc.), deer; and Perissodactyla (uneven-toed ungulates) consisting horse, ass, zebra, rhinoceros etc. The animals of this order are herbivorous in nature. Their role playing in the nature is as grazing animals and as chief prey animals to the carnivores, and thus have vital role in food-chain. They check overgrowth of various types of vegetations specially grasses. From the very beginning of the human civilization, the animals have been brought into the service of man and the breeds of cattle have been originated from the wild species serving a lot to the human-race from generation to generation. Besides these, many valuable things such as raw materials for woollen clothes from cheap to costliest are derived from wild sheeps and goats, beautiful furs of deer, musk, antlers and so many things of commercial value are gained from these animals which are of national and international trade value (by law, it is banned now). Deer are hunted for their meat, fur and antlers and that's why, they have come to threatened stage. The depletion in number of prey species leads the carnivores to be cattle-lifters or man-eaters as the alternative mode of food and, hence, man is harmed a lot. Ungulates serve as the largest terrestrial natural resource to man.

Pangolins and Man:

Pangolins (Scaly anteaters) belong to order Pholidota (formerly in order Edentata means without teeth) of class Mammalia. They are insect eaters particularly ants and termites having protrusible tongue. In this way, they help in maintaining the populations of such insects in nature which are harmful to crops and wooden materials. Thus, their role is important from eco-balance point of view.

Marine Mammals and Man:

Order Cetacea (whales, dolphins and porpoises) and Sirenia (sea-cows) under class Mammalia are the main marine mammals of Indian oceans. Dolphins are marine as well as freshwater such as gangetic dolphin. Marine mammals stand in second number as natural resource to man after terrestrial ungulates. They provide economic and commercial value to man as oil, fertilizer, fur, skin, fat etc. (presently hunting of wild animals is totally banned by law in India due to its alarming condition).

Birds and Man:

Relation between man and birds is well known since the dawn of our civilization. The majority of birds are serving as food to man from the time immemorable. So many species of singing and beautiful birds are pet since long back in human civilization. Their sweet song and mimic of version are world famous and man likes their association like parrot, mayna, koel etc. Peacock is famous for its beautiful feathers which is related with so many myths to keep in the house for welfare. History tells real miracle stories of pigeons acting as the messengers by carrying letters and reaching them to proper places. Majority of the species show social life with man. Maximum species are hunted for food (presently prohibited by law in our country). Most of the birds are insectivorous and are also prey of so many small carnivorous animals and thus play very important role in maintaining and balancing food-chain/food-web of the eco system. Some of them like vulture, eagle etc. are of scavenger nature playing great role in cleaning the environment making it pollution-free for us and others.

Reptiles and Man:

Reptiles specially crocodiles and muggar are of great importance to man. Their skin etc. are of great value leading them to be endangered due to illegal hunting. Snakes balance the population of rats in nature, though the venomous species are very harmful and fatal to man.

Fish and Man:

Number of varieties of edible marine and freshwater fishes are found serving as chief food for man all over the world. It is of great commercial as well as economic value to us. They are taken out from natural habitat and also cultured artificially to get more and more production on large scale. It is a great source of income and food fulfilling the high rate of man's food consumption. Now-a-days, fishery (pisciculture) has developed as an industry and the government of almost all countries have given much attention towards its propagation providing financial and technical assistance which is praiseworthy.

Man's activities have great influence on the lives of animals. Extermination of many species, as well as bringing most of them to the stage of extinction, are the resultant of man's activities. Though, carnivorous and herbivorous wild animals harm human life and properties including agricultural crops but their extermination is more harmful. For example, killing (extermination) of carnivorous animals such as weasels, stoats, badgers etc. in England to protect reared pheasants from their attack led to enormous increase in number of rabbits causing serious damage to crops and soil. Likewise, result is found with removal of other species like birds etc. by enhancing population of its prey and causing more damage than its predator. It is well established fact that each and every animal including beasts of prey have a definite role in the economy and balance of nature as well as natural resources. The necessity is to take steps to keep safe and undisturbed their habitats and manipulate, if required, as per need to provide sufficient food and shelter to the wild animal species so that they cannot feel or require to exploit men or sources of his food. The wild animals do such harms only in the scarcity of their food-supply or in case of human-interference with their food supplies or shrinkage of the habitats. Hence, exploitation of their food supplies by man greatly affects the ways and habits of these animals. Today, to live hormoniously, lovely and friendly with the wild animals making balance, is the prime demand of our duty and morality.

Chapter 6

Man and Wild Animal Conflict

Man appeared on this earth only about a million years ago. In the beginning, his needs were few because his culture, knowledge and other faculties were not fully developed. Then, he gradually started gaining superiority over other organisms by viture of his intelligence. Man has mastered the art of fulfilling some of his basic needs by artificial methods. He soon learnt the art of controlling and modifying the environment for his own comforts. With the development and advancement in science and technology, his standard of living and needs gradually started increasing and increasing. He made tools to fight and hunt wild animals. He learnt techniques of cultivation and started growing food for himself. He also started domesticating useful animals for milk, meat, egg, wool etc. He cleared forest to make houses, cities, industries, roads, bridges, dams, agricultural fields, transportation, communication etc. With these developments, which other organisms could not develop, man started utilizing natural resources much more than the other animals for his advantages, welfare, comforts and easy-going life. For the existence of an organism, basically three factors such as food, water and shelter are required. Hence, for wild animals also these basic requirements play important role in their growth and propagation. Since, all these basic components are exclusively related with their habitats which are undergoing tremendous changes primarily by the man for his needs, encroachment of forest land for grazing and agricultural purposes due to mushroom growth in human population. Therefore, man's manipulation of environment for his needs or greedy needs is the most prevalent factor affecting wildlife habitat and consequently wildlife populations. The man's use of these natural resources in his own way unscientifically caused bad impact on the wildlife.

The exploitation of forest as well as wild animals can be said to be main reason of all sorts of problems. Greedy persons are always busy in taking illegal benefits and cheap money from the forests causing its damage and habitat of wildlife. Some people inhabiting forest areas also indulge in such illegal activities. As a result, both forest as well as wildlife crops are now at alarming stage and we are passing through the age of danger. Over-exploitation is a serious threat to the wildlife. Illegal hunting of wild animals is always unscientific done by smugglers, local people residing in and around the forest, and other greedy persons for their own benefits causing heavy loss in wildlife populations. Unless and until such activities are stopped, we cannot achieve our goal through wildlife management.

As stated above; habitats, which protect wild animals, are being converted for human settlements and other requirements. Migratory animals are much vulnerable to destruction of habitats because disturbance at any point of their migratory routes affect them. Some of the dams are blocking spawning, migration of fishes by inundating the habitats and by altering the physical environment. Sometimes, a habitat may be damaged without significantly changing its physical appearance. For instances, the California Condor, the largest flying bird and a shy scavenger, is the victim of many human activities as well as severely affected by human cleanliness of its habitat such as the carcasses of livestock which form its food used to be left in the open in the past, but are presently buried or burnt. The introduction of exotic species deliberately or inadvertently has affected many native species by imposing new factors in competition for food, space, predation, habitat destruction, transmission of diseases, parasites and so on. The native species of fish of freshwater and of islands are specially affected by the introduction of new species. For example, exotic trout and bass endangered many species of fish in U.S.A. Goats and rabbits introduced in the islands of the Pacific and Indian Oceans have destroyed the habitats of several plants, birds and reptiles. The American chestnut trees found in the coastal areas of the U.S.A. have been devastated by a fungus (blight) introduced from China. Over-fishing is seriously depleting the marine living resources and significantly affecting the freshwater ones. Many species of fish, molluscs, whales, sea-cows, sea turtles etc. are going towards extinction as they are caught by mechanical devices for the sea-food industry. Due to over-exploitation, Cheetah, Sikkim Stag, Mountain quail, Pinkheaded duck are examples which have become extinct in India in recent times and many others are on the verge of extinction.

The importance and essentiality of existence of wild animals in respect of eco-balance and human-race have been dealt in the previous chapters. It is clear to understand that wild animals are the integral part of the ecosystem performing vital role in maintaining food-chain and food-web. Their existence and survival on the earth planet is much important and essential not only for natural-balance but also for the existence of human-life. It is well-established fact that the concern of wildlife is the concern for man himself. All forms of lives viz. human, animal and plant are so closely interlinked that disturbance in any one gives rise to imbalance in others. If species of plants or animals become endangered, they signify degradation in the environment which may threaten man's own existence. In these delicate interrelationship, the existence of one organism is dependent upon the other. The process of "natural selection" has led to species specializing in the performance of certain functions in food-chains. Destruction of any particular link in the chain may lead to imbalances which may threaten the existence of man himself on this planet. Nature maintains this vast diversity of animals and plants in a complex organization in which the various life processes of production, consumption and disposal of waste are maintained in well-balanced cycles. Plants and animals constitute the world's living resources and the various food-chains and cycles constitute life-support systems, essential for their survival, including the survival of man. To be sustainable, it is necessary that the renewability of the natural resources and life-support system is maintained in perpetuity. We cannot imagine well-beings of mankind without the optimum survival of every kind of wild species. Unfortunately, the renewable natural resources have been and being expoited by the man unscientifically as well as carelessly without thinking its adverse consequences. Since India is a developing country facing so many problems majorly tremendous growth in human population followed by poverty, unemployment, illiteracy and unawareness towards wildlife and nature; and hence selfishness for commercial exploitation as well as ornamental purposes, habitat destruction and illegal hunting for various purposes are the main reasons of depletion in wildlife population.

Merciless killings of wild animals and shrinkage of their habitats have resulted dwindling in population of wild animals facing problem of under-population being endangered/threatened and many are on the verge of extinction surpassing the stage of critical-limit and extinction of many important species of fauna and flora has taken place. Today, we are seeing disturbed ecosystem and life-support system before our eyes and, if left unchecked, it will be beyond our hands. It has been very correctly said that no natural resource is more sensitive to conservation than wildlife and no natural resource has suffered more from lack of conservation. The human-race has a long record of shameful over-exploitation of the earth's natural resources specially wildlife and large number of species had been made extinct and endangered. There are so many examples in this regard in different countries including India. Habitat changes brought about by man and over-killings of the species are reducing the numbers of wild animal species. In India, maximum wild animals are endangered and on the verge of extinction while cheetah, twohorned rhinoceros, mountain quil, pinkheaded duck are now extinct in this country. The upland plover and longbilled curlew birds in U.S.A. reduced their numbers due to combined actions of destroying their nesting grounds by grazing and ploughing, and overshooting. The wood duck was restored here by applying protection measure; because protection has a chance to restore wildlife where natural habitat remains available, but it cannot save species that no longer have suitable environment. Long back; egret, snowy heron, roseate spoonbill and other birds being on the verge of extintion by excessive killing, were brought back in great numbers by protection. Hence, it is clear that there are various causes for the decline of species, however, habitat disturbance and over-exploitation/illegal hunting of the species are the supreme ones.

Under multiple land-use planning (as described in chapter-4) and soil as well as water conservation practices, wildlife conservation programme should be tagged logically to propagate and compensate specialized habitats from wildlife point of view. The exact approach depends upon the type of land but in general it must fit for certain necessary and valuable wild animal species. Wildlife affects man and his interests in many ways, and his policy towards animals is influenced by their relationships to him. It may be based on real/fake facts, tradition or superstition. Man recognizes his dependence on the plants and animals for food, clothing and other needs. Though, considerations of cultivated and domestic forms belong to man but his relationship to the undomesticated and untamed forms (wildlife) is an important conservation work in the field of natural resources. From biological point of view, there are no beneficial and no harmful plants or animals in the world. All are long fitted in the great and miracle biological mechanism, one having its function upon other. All play their part in the complex natural processes including soil building and its fertility upon which plants grow and animals live on. It is, therefore, vitally necessary to man's interests that the natural process be kept at work properly by allowing communities of plant and animal life to exist and thrive on every piece of land even not needed for any other purposes. Therefore, classification of animals and plants as beneficial or injurious is not fundamentally biological, but usually on the basis of economic and aesthetic sense. On this basis, species are classified according to their real or supposed effects on man's interests. Thus, it is better to handle soil, water, forests and wildlife. It is useless to cry for past mistakes except with the aim to avoid similar errors in future. Now, the prime objective should be to repair damage as far as possible and put natural constructive process to work. In Indian condition, any managemnt plan for its wildlife must take into account the prevailing political and economic spheres, which is mainly governed by the marginal status of agriculture in the country. Therefore, the idea of wildlife as a crop should undoubtedly find a place in forest management in India. The problem behind it in the country is to save the fauna from disappearing or being reduced to the point of "no return" while at the same time ensuring to the cultivator adequate protection from crop damage and carnivorous animals. Since wildlife is an integral part of the land and, hence, must share in the various forms of land-utilization. In this way, wildlife also demands place in agricultural tracts under multiple land-use planning concept, though this aspect poses itself in our managed areas viz. reserved and protected forests. In India, the main impact on wildlife is on the cultivated and grazing lands where the existing contradictions must be resolved becasue today in the country it appears to be a major clash between wildlife-use and human-use of the land for cultivation. Though, it is essential that the cultivator should have proper liberty to defend his property from wild animals, it is equally essential that there should be certain areas or reserves where the shooting of wild animals is regulated and where the laws for their protection are rigidly enforced. Of course, the ceration of such reserve or national park will support in bringing the best status to the wild animals. It is essential to draw the attention of the people of the country in the direction of the magnificent heritage, gifted by nature, to realize the necessity for preserving and conserving them for their own benefits as well as for the coming generations.

To fulfil the mission, education will play vital role in bringing better position that what we are at present. Hence, it is needed to create such public opinion in our country on the subject of wildlife protection because today such opinion is not popularized and hardly exists in some quarters that are also not so active due to lack of proper interest and sufficient teaching. By applying modern management techniques, we can get economical profit.

As far as silvicultural operations of the forests are concerned; these should also be done wisely, carefully and scientifically after thorough studies for the sake of wild animals, and should not be with closed eyes following only traditional systems because the time and situation have changed a lot and, therefore, now requires modifications in such systems to be suitable as per the demand of the situations from both forests as well as wild animals point of view to cope the operational systems with the wild animals for their propagation in right direction to achieve the missions and objectives. It can be understood by the following facts. In planting a forest area, there should be burned or cut-over area of about ten acres to be left unplanted so that the trees developed might be interspersed with openings having a variety of vegetation available to wild animals. With the aim to get sustained-yield from forests, primarily two methods viz. selective and clear-felling systems are adopted. The selective system involves continuous selection of tree throughout the forest to be felled of commercial value and, thus, creates opening in the canopy encouraging growth of new ground vegetation which is better for many wild animal species. The clear-felling system involves clear cutting of block trees throughout the forest area each year as per the age-class available in smaller and widely scattered openings with breaking up of forests into blocks of trees of different age-classes often provides ideal food and cover for certain wild animals. The clear-cut areas in short time resume annuals and perennials vegetations adding variety of food to the certain wild animals. When complete cutting cycle is over, its annual production of food tends to avoid abrupt changes in animal populations caused by varying food supplies. Distribution of cuttings is also of considerable significance from wildlife point of view. Since the area is cut each year and if it is in contiguous to that cut the year before, there will be tendency to concentrate the wild animals exactly as in the case of the previous cut-over area. Such a condition will probably help in building up of various wild animals species, and their abrupt decline also when the area grows back into forest being less productive to the wild animals. It also depends upon the length of cutting-cycle as per the requirement of the animal species and food-supply in different situations. In case of natural clearings/fellings of forest trees creating openings hither and thither due to insects, diseases, wind, nongrowth of trees left as vacant spaces on rocks and unfertile soil etc. is of great importance providing ground vegetations of food and cover for specific wild animal species as well as their adequate distribution throughout the forest. Too intensive forestry, that is suppressing trees and shrubs of inferior commercial value, tends to reduce the variety of vegetations that support wild animals because improvement of valuable trees by cutting out less valuable may affect the future abundance of certain wild animals in such forest; and if drastic, it may greatly reduce or alter the populations also. Therefore; on the above facts, the work of planning needs care to be taken in such a way that it may not harm wild animals alongwith the improvement of the forest. The policy should fit in developing relationship between both wildlife and forestry crops.

In view of the above description, it is clear that habitat-destruction is the main reason of all sorts of problems due to human-interference in case of wild animals. As far as negative value of wild animals is concerned such as destruction of properties, taking lives of human-beings and livestock, damaging agricultural crops, predation, carriers of various diseases etc. the conflict between man and wild animal is arising and progressing day by day resulting primarily due to habitat-destruction and ongoing continuous shrinkage of habitats. For instance, in certain places now-a-days particularly in Jharkhand state, there is lot of problem of elephants due to invading village areas destroying agricultural crops, houses, properties and even lives of people in more or less large scale. Villagers are always afraid and suspicious of such notorious activities of the animal. Conversion of forest land into agricultural fields, illegal hunting, unsustainable development, land clearing, settlement etc. increasingly threaten the few remaining wild Asiatic elephants and such activities led to man-elephant conflict. Therefore, a crucial factor in the survival of both the species (man and elephant) is the availability of large enough areas to be managed sustainably meeting the demands of both human and animal populations. The habitat-destruction through the forest conversion to other land-uses has created great pressure on elephant. As a resultant, the elephants move down, specially in dry season, from forest to the local farmers' crops and their houses for food. Number of elephants as well as villagers have become victims and killed in protecting crops and struggling each other. The problem is increasing day by day. Crops and lives of the farmers are destroyed while elephants are being shot, poisoned or maimed or electrocuted. Thus, the threats of man-elephant has become a challening task for government and officials. To overcome the problem, it is necessary to conduct survey with the co-operation of people living in and around elephant habitat regarding population, food source, water source, habitat position, position of migratory routes, dangers etc. It is also essential to create awareness among people towards protection of wild elephants coming together with the government officials and other agencies. In this way, a concrete plan of conservation strategies saving and protecting the existence of both man and elephant benefitting each other may be established developing sound land-use patterns to remove confrontations. The needs of both humans and elephants must compete with the limited resources of the land. There must be a balance between both the species in sustainable and perpetual manner. Since elephants need extensive areas to survive and reproduce successfully, the fragmentation and eventual loss of the habitat is the main threat to the elephants as stated above. If such situation of habitat-destruction and improper management persists, the day is not far when the carnivorous animals like tiger, lion, panthers, hyaena etc. may also indulge themselves in such damaging activities being cattle-lifter and man-eater all over the country; because when anybody destroys the one's house, it is obvious to be violent against the destroyer who made him homeless. So, there is another face of wildlife problem emerging now-a-days that is the increasing/increased number of many species of wild animals which became man-eaters/killers and cattle killers/crop eaters in nearby villages. For example as stated above, elephants in the states of Assam, Jharkhand etc. have killed and killing so many people and raid the agricultural crops as well as damaging domestic properties. The tigers of Sunderbans have become man-eaters. Tigers are also inserting such problem by killing the people and lifting the cattle. Though, lion in Gir forest is not much in number but are also wandering out of the reserve area causing damage. Crocodiles, released in the rivers, attack the fish population. Nilgai and wild ass in Rajasthan always raid the crops of the villagers. People are being victims of such phenomenon and the local people are raising their voices against such mishappenings. Such people are becoming anti-conservationinsts and the cases of poisoning the animals are coming into pictures. It has become national problem and a big headache to the governments as well as forest officials. But such problem arose/arising due to insufficient habitat. On one hand, the population of a species became enhanced by applying conservation/protection measures, but at the same time on the other hand, the proper management of the habitat as per the demand of the carrying-capacity of the population of the species was not done rightly. There must be synchronization between population-enhancement of the species, and carrying-capacity of the habitat. For this, proper management/manipulation in the habitat is the most essential aspect, otherwise such type of situation is inevitable and cannot be checked. It is to be noted that local abundance of a species does not mean that it is out of danger, but it means that its present habitat is not sufficient and is mismanaged. Hence, real problem lies in the management and planning of the reserve or habitat. The actual scenario is that most of the India's wild animals are pushed into nearly only 5 percent areas of the national parks and sanctuaries of the country's geographical area, and even these forest areas have also been/being encroached by the villagers. Traditional corridors which enabled the animals to move from one forest to another have been cut off. Even the protected national parts and sanctuaries are not free from human-disturbance/intrusion and cattle grazing. Even in core-zones of most of the parks and sanctuaries, people are residing. Most of the buffer-zones have disappeared and fringes of these have turned into major battle ground between man and wild animals.

Seeing the present status of wild animals and situation of the people, following measures must be adopted-

i) Careful analysis of conservation techniques applied for the species concerned.
ii) Evaluation of carrying-capacity of the habitat and its management/manipulation accordingly.
iii) Census should be carried out regularly.
iv) Regular monitoring and management should be carried out.
v) Establishment of more Protected Areas/Biosphere Reserves should be developed.
vi) Alternative habitats for rare and endangered species.
vii) Establishment of Game Breeding Farm for rare and endangered species.
viii) Species from overstocked areas should be translocated to understocked areas.
ix) Control of exotic species.
x) Adequate planning for pest control.
xi) Captive Breeding for rare and endangered species.
xii) Carrying-capacity of human population residing in and around the wildlife habitats should be studied and alternative engagement of earning should be provided to them to check the pressure on forest, wild animals and their habitats (forest and nonforest habitats).

xiii) Shifting of people from Protected Areas providing them adequate facilities.

xiv) Creation of awareness towards importance of wildlife and its conservation among the general mass.

Hence, habitat management is as important as wildlife conservation. The wildlife manager must identify those factors which affect the habitat, specially which do not design or implement for wildlife, and must understand the interrelationship between the animal and the habitat. For example, in U.S.A. it has been found that the dense old growth forests may be disastrous to the spotted owl's nesting and feeding requirements while it greatly increases preferred forage food for elk. There are many examples for the manipulated environment to be beneficial or detrimental to wildlife. It is the responsibility of wildlife manager to judge how such practices should be modified to enhance habitat-diversity for proper growth and propagation of wild animal being suitable for individuals and productivity of the species. Thus, the most serious threat to and from the wild animals comes from habitat destruction. A basic consideration should be the balance between mortality and reproduction. Some of the endangered forms are handicapped by having a naturally low reproductive-rate. Though; under optimum conditions, this may be of no great disadvantage, but it can create serious repercussions if normal reproduction is checked by undue disturbance or by such factors as weakening of a species-vitality through fragmentation of the population.

Chapter 7

Decimating Factors of Wild Animals

There are many factors of death of an organism. If death becomes at old age means covering the individual's life-span at which the cells of the body become exhausted, inactive and functionless showing physiological break-down; it is called natural death. It is natural, sure and certain phenomenon of each and every living organism. But, on the contrary, if there is death due to some factor/factors other than natural as stated above, it is called uncommon/ premature death or unnatural death and the causal factor responsible for such death is known a decimating factor. In case of wildlife, due to decimating factor or environmental factor or environmental resistance or over-production or excess number beyond the carrying capacity of the habitat, such uncommon death of the individuals occurs before the old age viz. before covering full life-span. Hence, decimating factors play great role in the growth of a population and determining direction and speed of population-dynamics of a species. In other words, it can be said that population-growth may be raised by decreasing decimating factors and increasing natality-rate of a species. The objective of wildlife management is to minimize the effects of such decimating-factors to reduce mortality-rate. In general, decimating-factors may be categorized in following heads -

(1) Adverse Climate : Due to adverse climatic conditions such as very hot weather, excessive rainfall, flood, draught, excess cold, earthquake, volcano etc., casualty in wild animals occurs causing loss of lives when the condition becomes beyond the tolerance/resistance capacity of the individuals/species concerned. However, the population having excess number of individuals than the carrying-capacity of its habitat is more liable to such deaths because they become unable to bear even minor changes in the habitat having less resistance. Such deaths can be minimized by increasing carrying-capacity as well as fundamental requirements (food, water and shelter) through habitat and population manipulations by applying scientific technologies after thorough research and findings.

(2) Accidents : In wildlife, accidents generally occur due to fire, flood, drought, volcano, earthquake, road-crossing etc. causing death. Therefore, proper management and care are required to check such accidents to save wildlife species.

(3) Poisoning : Though, the wild animals have their own natural instinct power to avoid poisonous materials to take in but poisoning through man is much dangerous causing causality. Such practices is found common in our country adopted by the villagers/farmers to protect agricultural crops, cattle, domestic commodities and their own lives. Under man-animal conflict, killing of carnivores, herbivores including elephants is happening oftenly. Problems are from both the sides. Wild animals are also compelled to invade towards village areas in and around the habitat due to habitat-destruction/shrinkage followed by habitat-fragmentation and encroachment/destruction of corridors. Likewise; men, as resentment, are also doing mischievous activities by poisoning and killing the wild animals. It is very essential to control such activities legally as well as by persuation and consciousness; and simultaneously, habitat-manipulation in proper way in accordance with the population for its sustenance is very much necessary to check and control the damage and casualty caused by wild animals. The situation should be thought from both the angles and remedial measures must be applied very honestly, wisefully, judiciously and scientifically to get the fruitful result within the shortest period so that both the species (human and wild) may live and grow peacefully in their own houses (habitats).

(4) Illegal hunting : To get cheap money; the greedy persons living in and around the forest, smugglers and others are indulged in doing illegal hunting and poaching of wild animals which is always unscientific. Without stopping such activities, proper wildlife management cannot be done and goals cannot be achieved. This should be stopped by legal measures as well as by educating and creating awareness among general mass towards the importance of conservation of wild animals regarding its role played in eco-balance and for the existance of human race.

(5) Stress : It is the natural phenomenon that after reaching to the stage of optimum-density/subsistence density in a population; loss in its number of individuals starts due to excess number than the carrying-capacity of the habitat, although enough availability of basic needs (food, water and shelter) is found in the habitat. A kind of stress in imposed upon the population to counterbalance the nature for bringing eco-balance in that habitat resulting death of certain excess numbers of the population under stress. Though, the actual reason of such stress resulting death comes due to the intraspecific-competition and excess contact among them in which adrenal-pituitary system is disturbed arising endocrine-imbalance secreting excess quantity of hormones and disturbing feed-back mechanisms and ultimately death of the individuals. Hence, to increase carrying-capacity of the habitat through proper management techniques is also required to minimize such stress.

(6) Starvation : Sometimes due to certain reasons or changes in the habitat, the animals get obstacles in feeding. Such conditions compel them to go on starvation, and it the period prolongs, the animals become very weak and ultimately die. It is generally found in carnivorous animals due to reduction in number of the herbivores. Therefore, the appropriate measures must be tried to avoid the conditions causing starvation.

(7) Movement : Since the wild animals are always mobile in search of food, water etc. and during its movement the individuals get death especially when the population migrate from one habitat to the another.

(8) Predation : Under prey-predator relationship, the carnivores are always in search of its prey to satisfy its instinctive needs of food as per the preferred choice. The series of energy-transfers through the food-chain/food web is linked with one to the other and ends in a predator which has no enemies. Predators have an important role in regulation "balance of nature". If predation does not exist, the biological pressure of expansion of an organism would soon result in giving no space for other life and multiplication of a species is automatically controlled by predation, disease and other decimating factors. Predation varies with the number of animals in excess of the capacity of the environment to support them that is with the fluctuation between biological -pressure and environmental-resistance. Generally, predators live on annual surplus produced by a prey species, but when predation departs from the normal phenomenon of losses among the less vigorous and instead takes place among the more vigourous classes, a weakness or breakdown of the environment is indicated. Predator control may give benefit to a desired species on areas where other environmental conditions are favourable for increase, particularly when the number of the prey species are below the normal. Thus, control efforts need to be specific for the target predator and emphasis should be upon control of damage rather than upon control of predators. There is need for the recognition of many values of the predators and caution and careful direction in control. Therefore, proper and better identification of predators is to be classified as truly destructive and requiring control, because in nature the biological balance represents the evolutionary adjustment between breeding potential and environmental-resistance/ decimating factors. When these two opposite forces remain in balance, the population remains static. But when they become imbalanced, there is gain or loss in wildlife population; because if the biotic-potential of the species is more than that of the resistance, there will be growth in the population and *vice versa*. Productivity tends to decrease with increase of abundance and to increase with decrease of numbers.

(9) Human-interference : The illegal and unscientific exploitation of forest crop as well as wildlife crop can be said as the main root of all sorts of problems. The greedy persons are always busy to get cheap money through illegal benefits causing damage to the forest and wild animals including its habitats. As the consequences, we are passing through the age of danger. Interference by man adopting illegal activities is damaging both wild fauna and flora bringing the situation at alarming stage. Proper hard rules and its unbiased implementation are required to control the situation and save the natural heritage. But at the same time, alternative means of earning/engagement to the people residing in and around the forest habitat should be provided to minimize or nullify the pressure on forest and wild animals. The Wild Life (protection) Act, 1972 has become an effective approach which is being amended from time to time as per the demand of the situation. CITES, IUCN and other national and international organizations have proved affirmative results. But despite all these laws and rules, illegal trade and killings of wildlife is continuing and even flourishing. It is the demand of the time to thinkover the gravity of this alarming situation of wildlife and implement the remedial measures removing all types of anomalies. As far as cruelty and crimes appendex to wild animals are concerned, it is done by so many means. The major method is smuggling them in live forms or their products and commodities getting high commercial value in the international market and also consumption as meat whereever possible. It is done generally by fake and misdeclaration of the article, hiding and concealment of the material, false permit, false claim, adulterating the original material and so on. Likewise, methods of killing/poaching are by using pit, hunting, poisoning, electrocution, snaring, netting, sticking in rod by the help of glue, capturing/killing by sharp pointed iron device attached on the tip of rod, harpooning, collecting young from nests of birds, trawling, by digging to capture underground animals etc. In this way, there are various ways and means to capture or kill wild animals for the purposes of smuggling and consumption. In this respect, there should be tight surveillance and patrolling, antipoaching team, experts to detect original materials concealed/adulterated particularly fur, horns, antlers, body parts, bones etc. There should be accurate and just planning behind it. Hence, it can be said that human interference in case of wild animals is a challenging task and unless it is checked and controlled, the up-to-mark propagation of the species concerned is not possible.

(10) Diseases : Wild animals are suffering from various types of diseases which act as important decimating factor. A lot of loss is caused by them and in case of wild animals, it is difficult to diagnose and treat them in time because they are free-ranging animals as well as hiding themselves in core area of the habitat. It is better to apply preventive measures to check epidemic condition to protect the population, however, it is also necessary to treat them properly after suffering from the disease. Modern techniques evolving day by day for identifying the individuals and its health-checking should be adopted to avoid further complications and minimize speed of the disease. The diseases caused in the wild animals are from different sources of parasites and pathogens. Some are infectious, some are through pathogens like bacteria, virus, protozoan, helminths etc., some arise through contaminated food and water, and some spreading through the cattle which is most prevalent. Apart from this, the diseases which are transmissible between animals and men, called as zoonoses, are of great importance because such diseases are transmitted from wildlife (wild fauna) to man and animals. The other reverse process is transmission of diseases from man to domestic animals to the wild animals. Therefore, socio-economic aspect of man has direct relation especially with the rural people because their cattle always intrude in the territory of wild animals for grazing. Since wildlife is the mirror of the health of the environment, their conservation and protection is an important and essential component from environmental and natural-balance point of view; and the aspect regarding control of diseases in both natural and artificial habitats (in-situ & ex-situ) plays vital of this field. India has a diversified range of climate from tropical to temperate and desert including humid and dry conditions, their management needs through studies and proper application of techniques, because unfortunately the wild animals has come or have been brought to the alarming stage, specially in developing countries, resulting endangered/threatened/rare situation including extinction of so many species due to habitat alterations, human interference/activities and disease. Some of the important diseases may be categorized as follows –

(A) In fishes :

(a) Fungal diseases :-

1. **Gill Rot** - This disease is caused by the fungus *Brachiomyces sanguinis* which infects gills of fishes and obstructs veins of gill filaments. The diseased fish shows red flackings on gill filaments becoming greyish-white in later stage and finally drop off. The fish dies by suffocation.

2. **Ulcer** - It is caused by the fungus namely *saprolegnia parasitica.* There is ulceration and haemorrhage on the skin, blindness and inflammation of liver and intestine. On the infected site of the skin, white hair like outgrowths of fungus may be observed.

(b) Bacterial diseases :-

1. **Fin and Tail Rot** - The diseases is caused by bacteria

badly affecting pisiculture industry. White lines appear on the margin of affected fin which finally disintegrates. It is an infectious disease.

2. **Ulceration** - In this disease which is caused by bacteria, ulceration on the skin and muscle of fish appears and increases gradually.

3. **Dropsy** - It is caused by Aeromonas bacteria in carps. There is accumulation of fluid inside body cavity, protrusion of scales and inflammation of intestine.

4. **Eye-diseases** - The bacteria *Aeromonas liquefaciens* and *Staphylococcus aureus* cause infection of eyes, optic nerves and even brain and finally eye ball in putrefied resulting death of the fish. Such cataract like condition is commonly found in catla and channa.

(c) Protozoan diseases :-

1. ***Ichthyopthiriasis* (White spot)** - It is caused by protozoa called as *Ichthopthirius multifilis* affecting skin, gills, fins and other external parts of the carps. Small whitish spots are seen over the infected organ.

2. **Myxosporidian disease** - Myxosporidians like Leptotheca, Chloromyxum, Myxobolus, Henneguya, Thelohanellus, Myxidium and Lentospera cause infection in fishes resulting loss of scales and chromatophores on the skin. The scales may be perforated or raised.

Apart from these, certain species of Elimeria infect liver, kidney etc., species of Cryptobia and Microspora etc. are responsible for infecting gills and vascular system; whereas species of Plistophora and Glugea etc. cause infection in muscle and cartilage; Nosema species infect control nervous system; Plistophora etc. cause reproductive system infection; and some of the Costia, Ciliophora etc. give rise to infections on skin and subcutaneous tissue of the fishes.

(d) Helminthic diseases

1. **Trematodal diseases** - Trematodes such as Gyrodactylus, Dactylogyrus, Genarchopsis, Allocreadium, Diplostomum, Benedenia, Crepidostromum, Sanguinicola etc. infect skin, gills, internal organs etc. of fishes causing death.

2. **Cestodal diseases** - Among cestodes which generally infect fishes are Lytocestus, Bothriocephalus, Crescentrovittus, Caryophyllaeus, Protocephallus, Triaenophorus, Diphylobothrium, Ligula etc. infect interval organs, skin, gills etc. of the fishes causing their casualty.

3. **Nematodal disease** - The nematodes which cause infection among fishes are mainly Procamallanus, Neocamallanus, Paracamallanus, Indocamallanus, Heliconema, Proleptus, Zeylanema, Capillaria etc. They infect various parts of internal organs of fishes and results heavy losses.

4. **Acanthocephalous diseases** - Majorly Neochinorhynclus, Acanthocephalus, Acanthogyrus, Pallisentis, Echinortynchus, Pomphorhynchus etc. worms infect fishes and their tissues.

5. **Crustacean disease** - Some species of crustacea and leaches act as ectoparasites on the body of fishes such as Argulus, Lernaea, Ergasilus etc. and lead to bacterial and fungal infections.

(B) In Amphibia :

The amphibians like frogs etc. are infected by many bacteria and viruses such as Aeromonus, Pseudomonas, Chlamydis etc. They also get infection through protozoan and helminthic parasites such as Ganeo, Mehraorchis, Tremiorchis, Halipegus etc. causing metabolic disorders.

(C) In Reptilia :

(a) **Bacterial & Viral disease** - Numerous respiratory diseases are caused by bacteria and virus in reptiles. Pneumonia and Stomatis are caused by bacteria in snakes whereas Entobacterial infections are found in other reptiles. Gangrenous pneumonia is caused by Aspergillus, Beauveria and Poecilomyces in reptiles.

(b) **Protozoan disease** - Among protozoans, the common amoebic pathogens are Entamoeba, Dsopora and Eimeria causing infection in snakes, lizards, tortoises, crocodiles etc. arising amoebiasis. Besides these, the protozoans such as Trypanosoma, Leishmania, Trichomonas, Hexamita, Tritrichomonas, Monocercomonas, Coccidia, Haemosporidia, Plasmodium, Haemoproteus etc. cause infections in certain reptiles.

(c) **Trematodal disease** - Renifers, styphylodora, spirorchids etc. infect some of the reptiles especially gastro intestinal and circulatory systems.

(d) **Helminthic disease** - The helminths like Bilorchis, Paradistomum, Strongyluris, Oochoristica, Diphyllobothrides, Pseudophylliadae, Mescocestoides, Proteocephalidae, Ascaridae, Stronglylidae, Rhabditida, Oxyurides, Spirurida, Acanthocephalan etc. infect reptilian internal organs causing disorders in their systems.

In addition; leeches (Annelid), mites and ticks (Acarids) act as ectoparasites in reptiles and an arthropodan worm namely Raillietiella infects lungs of lizards and cause severe damage.

(D) In Birds :

(a) Viral diseases :-

1. **Laryngeotracheitis** - It is a common viral disease in birds showing gasping, coughing, nasal discharge and conjunctivitis. It is highly contagious found generally in crane, pigeon, fowl etc.

2. **Avian influenza** - Generally found in geese, pigeon, migratory birds, fowl etc. having respiratory problem, coughing and sneezing.

3. **Avian pox** - It is common viral disease in birds in which wart like nodules are formed over the body. Upper digestive and respiratory tract also become infected. Chicken, sparrow, pigeon, pheasants etc. are most victims.

4. **New castle disease** - Oftenly found in sparrow, pigeon, crane, crow, koel, domestic fowl etc. showing signs of listlessness, respiratory problem and watery greenish diarrhoea.

5. **Marek's disease** - It is found specially in captive pheasants showing lameless, paralysis and loss of weight.

(b) Fungal diseases :-

1. **Aspergillosis** - It is respiratory disease found in birds caused by fungus Aspergillus developing in air passage or lungs. Pheasants, pigeon, chicken geese etc. are generally victims of such infection.

2. **Thrush** - It is caused by *Candida albicans* growing in

digestive tract causing ulcer in crop and other parts of chicken, pigeon etc.

(c) Bacterial diseases :-

1. **Avian tuberculosis** - It is caused by *Micobacterium avium* in all species of birds but in more common in caged birds. It is highly contagious diseases and results in death.

2. **Avian cholera** - It is caused by *Pasteurella multocida* and *P. septica* in pheasants, turkey, water fowl, ducks etc.

3. **Avian coryza** - It is infectious disease caused by *Hemophilus gallinarum* found in sparrow, duck, pigeon, crane etc. having signs of nasal discharge, oedema of face, conjunctivitis with breathing problem.

4. **Pullorum** - It is caused by *Salmonella pullorum* infecting young birds specially sparrow, duck, pigeon, fowl etc. In advance stage, birds die suddenly.

5. **Fowl typhoid and paratyphoid** - It is infected by *Salmonella gallinarum* and *S. typhimuram* in fowl, swans, duck, turkey, sparrow etc. causing typhoid and paratyphoid respectively and results heavy mortality.

6. **Mycophasmosis** - It is respiratory tract disease caused by Mycoplasma found in owl, pheasants, pigeon etc.

7. **Erysipelas** - This is caused by *Erysipelothrix insidiosa* found generally in sparrow, turkey, parrots, pheasants etc. showing diarrhoea listlessness and anorexia. It is an infectious disease.

8. **Spirochaetosis** - It is an infectious disease caused by *Borrelia anserina* generally in doves, ducks, geese, pigeon, turkey etc. showing signs of fever, depression, diarrhoea and

paralysis.

9. **Staphylococcosis (Bumble foot)** - It is caused by *Staphylococcus auresu* bacteria generally found in pheasants. The disease is chronic in nature and birds become dull, off-fed, lame foot pad swollen containing white pus.

10. **Colisepticaemia** - The disease is caused by *Entamoeba coli* in pheasant showing off-fed, dull gasping, staggering gait and increased respiration.

(d) Protozoan diseases :-

1. **Trichomoniasis** - It is caused by *Trichomonas gallinae* parasite which infects mouth, oesophagus and head of hawks, pigeons etc. This disease may lead to the blindness in birds. Contaminated food and water are the cause of transmission of this disease among the birds.

2. **Coccidiosis** - This disease is caused by species of Coccidia in vulture, crane, pigeon, turkey, fowl etc. infecting intestinal wall of the birds.

3. **Histomoniasis** - It is caused by *Histomonas meleagridis* which infects liver and gut of chicken, turkey etc.

4. **Bird's malaria** - Plasmodium causes the disease in geegs, bulbul, turkey etc. which is transmitted by bite of mosquitoes like other hosts.

5. **Trypanosomiasis** - It is caused by species of Trypanosoma in owl, pigeon etc.

6. **Helminthic disease** - Several species of round worms, tape worms, flukes infect gut, respiratory tract, eyes and air sacs of duck, quail, turkey etc. Species of Capillaria, Gongylonema, Ascaridia, Heterakis, Davinea, Amoebotaenia,

Hymenolepis, Raillietina, Diplepis, Echinostoma, Euclinostomum, Prosthogonimus, Typhlocoelium, Philopthalmus, Polymorphus and Plagiorhynchus are notable in causing diseases in birds.

A number of ticks, mites, bugs and fleas also live as ectoparasites on the body of wild birds.

(E) In Mammals :

(a) Viral diseases :-

1. **Rabies** - It is caused by Rhabdo virus particularly Lyssa virus. It is very dangerous disease and found commonly in pet and street dogs, wolf, jackal, fox, mongoose, jungle cat, lion, tiger etc.

2. **Foot and Mouth Disease (FMD)** - The disease is caused by Picorna virus among hoofed mammals specially in artiodactyla. It is an infectious disease followed by cattle grazing in forest areas. Wild boar, cheetal, sambhar, gaur etc. are the most sufferers of this disease.

3. **Cat plaque** - It is caused by Parvo virus in tiger, leopard, jaguar, wild cat etc. The disease is characterized by fever, vomiting and diarrhoea.

4. **Measles** - It is caused by Paramyxo virus in monkeys giving sign of coughing, pneumonia and swelling of face.

5. **Rinderpest** - The disease is caused by Paramyxo virus (Morbilli virus) as epidemic in the ruminants such as cheetal, sambhar, gaur, wild buffalo, cattle etc. It is infected in wild animals through the cattle.

6. **Distemper** - It is found generally in carnivorous animals caused by Paramyxo virus affecting central nervous system

and signs like watering through eyes and nose, coughing, swelling in eyes and toes, dermatitis etc. Infection is caused through the materials oozing out from eyes and nose.

(b) Funtal disease :- Many species of fungi infect wild mammals. Microsporum causes ring worm disease in wild primates while Cryptococcus causes skin infections.

(c) Bacterial diseases :-

1. **Tuberculosis -** This disease is found in wild animals also like man. It is caused by *Bacterrium tuberculosis* infecting through food, water or air inside the body which is commonly found in monkey, deer, pig etc.
2. **Anthrax -** It is caused by Anthracis bacteria known as *Bacillus anthrasis* in wild herbivores causing enlargement of spleen.
3. **Brucellosis -** Brucella bacteria causes this disease in cattle, cheetal, sambhar etc. Infection is caused by food, water and wound. Tumor in the joints arises and foetus is also damaged.
4. **Botulism -** This disease is caused by *Clostridium botulinum.* It is a kind of paralysis caused by the consumption of poisonous food made by the bacteria. In severe condition, heart attack is caused due to paralysis and animal dies. It is very common in aquatic birds all over the world. Outwardly, it is observed that there is continuous tearing and all of sudden the flying bird drops and dies immediately.
5. **Leptospirosis -** It is caused by Leptospira generally in dogs. It is highly contagious and is transmitted through rats.
6. **Necorbacillosis -** It is a diseases of ruminants caused by *Fusiformis necrophorus* in which lesions are formed in soft

parts around the hoof.

7. **Diarrhoea and dysentry** - It is caused in most of the wild primates by Shigellosis, Salmonellosis, Yersiniosis, Aerobactor and Escherichia.

8. **Pneumonia** - In many wild primates, this disease is caused by Staphylococddi and Pneumococci infecting respiratory organs causing pneumonia.

(d) Protozoan diseases :-

1. **Trypanosomiasis** - It is caused by *Trypanosoma evansi* in tiger, leopard, jaguars etc.

2. **Coccidiosis** - It is commonly found in wild mammals. In carnivores, it is caused by Isopara whereas in ruminants by Eimeria. It is a chronic disease in which intestinal mucosa is damaged by the parasite and causes diarrhoea and haemorrhage in intestinal wall.

3. **Saroporidiosis** - It is caused by Sacrocystis in cattle, pigs, mice etc. and skeletal muscles are infected causing anaemia and abortion.

4. **Haemoprotozoan diseases** - Infection in wild primates is caused by Leishmania, Plamodium and Toxoplasma. Malaria in monkey is common.

5. **Amoebiasis** - In wild primates, the disease is caused by *Entamoeba histolytica, E. coli, Blantidium coli* and *Iodamoeba butschli* with the sign of diarrhoea and presence of blood mucus in stool.

(e) Helminthic diseases :- The diseases caused by worms in wild mammals are through Ancyclostoma, Riticularia, Spelotrema, Echinococcus, Trichenella, Ascaris, Toxocara,

Castrothylax, Amphistoma, Taenia, Moniliformis, Fasciola etc. Nilgai, jackal, lion, tiger, cheetal, sambhar, cattle etc. generally suffer by the infections of such helminths. The common disease caused by helminths in wild mammals are -

1. **Toxocariasis -** It is common in carnivores caused by nematode Toxocara showing ill growth and gastrointestinal problem.

2. **Hookworm disease -** It is common in wild mammals caused by Ancylostoma and Uncinaria having sign of weakness and anaemia.

3. **Hydatidosis -** It is common disease in ruminants caused by cestodes.

4. **Stenofilariasis -** Nilgai suffers from sores in ear due to this disease.

A number of ticks, mites and fleas live as ectoparasites on the body of wild mammals.

(f) Contaminated diseases :- Due to consumption of contaminated food or water, the wild mammals suffer from certain diseases such as -

1. **Haemorrhagic septicaemia -** It is an infectious diseases arising due to impurities of blood found in young hoofed animals like deer, boar, sheep, birds etc. It is common in the animals eating dirty food and water showing high fever, redness in eyes, throat swelling and hoarse voice.

2. **Black quarter -** Infectious disease generally found in young hoofed animals just after rainy season due to the consumption of dirty and stagnaut water.

In addition to the above, there are certain diseases which

are transmitted in wild mammals by the insects which act as carriers/vectors and infection is caused by the pest organisms.

Thus, it may be concluded that decimating factors play vital role in the growth of wild animals, and it is essential to understand and investigate those as well as to control and manage the same in proper way in the field of wildlife management so that objective aimed to the target species may be achieved as per the planned strategies within the specified period.

Index